THE HISTORY

DINGS

CRUSADERS

RUGBY CLUB

THE HISTORY OF
DINGS
CRUSADERS
RUGBY CLUB

A CLUB WITH ITS HEART IN BRISTOL

IAN HADDRELL

The
History
Press

First published 2017

The History Press
The Mill, Brimscombe Port
Stroud, Gloucestershire, GL5 2QG
www.thehistorypress.co.uk

British Library Cataloguing in Publication Data.
A catalogue record for this book is available from the British Library.

ISBN 978 0 7509 8419 5

Typesetting and origination by The History Press
Printed in Turkey by Imak Offset

CONTENTS

Dings R.F.C. Fixtures 1898-9

Date	Opponent	Ground	Result	For	Against
Oct 1	Elton St Michaels	their ground	E.St.M 5 tries Dings 1 goal		
Oct 8	No game	—	—		
" 15	St Marys 2nd	their ground	St Mary 1 try Dings 1 goal	5 / 5	15 / 3
" 22	M.V.Tech. College F.C	their ground	M.V. nil Dings nil	Draw	
" 29	St Agnes 3rd	their ground	St Agnes 1 goal Dings 1 try	3	5
Nov 5	Avonmouth 2nd	our ground	No game	0	0
" 12	Mr V. Tech: College F.C	our ground	M.V. nil Dings nil	0	0
" 19	Kempes School	their ground	Kempes 2 gls 1 try Dings 1 goal	5	13
" 26	St Mary 2nd	our ground	St Mary 2 nd tries Dings	0	9
Dec 3	No game	—	—		
" 10	St Agnes Juniors	their ground	St Agnes nil Dings 1 d gl 2 tries	10	0
" 17	Avonmouth 2nd	their ground	Avonmouth 2 goals Dings 1 try	3	10
" 24	Eversley 3rd	our ground	Eversley 3 nil Dings 10 tries	30	0
" 31	Eversley 2nd	their ground	Dings 1 try from Eversley 1 goal free kick	3	3
Jan 7 1899	St Agnes 3rd	our ground	Dings nil points St Agnes 7 tries	0	7
" 14	Bishopston Wesley guild	our ground	Bis Wes: guild nil Dings 2 tries	6	0
" 21	Belgrave Athletic 2nd	their ground	Belgrave 1 try Dings 1 goal 1 try	8	3
" 28	M V Tech: College	their ground	MVT C. nil Dings 1 goal 1 try	8	0
Feb 4	Belgrave Athletic 2nd	our ground	no game		
11	St Mary 2nd	"	Dings nil St Mary 2nd nil	0	0
18	St Agnes 3rd 2nd	our ground	Dings 2 tries St Agnes 1 goal	6	5
25	Bath Y.M.C.O. 1st	our ground	Dings 1 goal YMCA nil	5	0
Mch 4	Elton St Michaels	our ground	Dings 1 goal E. St Michaels nil	5	0
Mch 11	Eversley 2nd	our ground	Dings 6 tries Eversley 2nd 1 try	18	3
" 18	Dings 2nd	their ground	Dings 2 2 1g 1 try	0	8
Mch 25	Bishopston Wesley guild	their ground	Bishopston nil Dings 26 points	26	0
Aprl 3	Oakfield 2nd	their ground	draw	0	0

Handwritten contemporaneous Dings Crusaders fixture list for season 1898/99, which includes the results of the matches. Interestingly, on Christmas Eve Dings beat Eversley Thirds 30–0, scoring ten tries, none of which were converted into goals.

ACKNOWLEDGEMENTS

This book could not have been written without the help and advice of many people, the majority of whom have either played for or been associated with Dings Crusaders RFC. A big thank you to all those past and present members of 'Dings' – many of whom appear in the pages of this book – without whose contribution of photographs, memorabilia and memories of a unique club this history would not have been possible. I am indebted to you all.

I also owe a debt of gratitude to the late Bob Beynon for his meticulous record keeping of all Dings-related matters, and the late Ron Lloyd for his preservation of equally meticulous records and a comprehensive newspaper cutting library. A special thank you to Harry Phillips for his assistance in the production and copying of the club's historic photographs, the taking of contemporary pictures, and his unstinting persistence in requesting artefacts and memorabilia from all and sundry at the club.

In addition, I would like to acknowledge the assistance given by Sandy Mitchell, the doyen of the Bristol Combination, for providing me with access to the Bristol & District Combination committee minutes and the historical Bristol & District Combination Handbooks.

My biggest thank you, however, goes to Steve Lloyd, who has been associated with Dings for well over forty years as player, captain and since 1998 chairman, for his support of the project, his tolerance of my incessant questions and requests for information, and his willingness to loan me many precious and unique Dings Crusaders archives and records.

With thanks to: Avonmouth Old Boys RFC, Avon Sports Photography, *Bath Chronicle*, Bert Angell, Barton Hill History Group, Bishopston RFC, Richard Boddie, Ray Bowden, Pete Boyes, Bristol & District Combination, *Bristol*

Evening Post, *Bristol Mercury*, Bristol Record Office, Bristol Reference Library, Bristol United Press, Patrick Casey, Sue Chappell, Tony Collins, Helga Fox, *Gloucestershire Citizen*, *Gloucestershire Echo*, Alan Grant, Richard Grant, Mark Hoskins, Peter Lawson, Elizabeth Leaming (*née* Brooks), Brenda LLewellin (*née* Pavey), Dave Lucas, Phil McCheyne Photographers, Helen Meller, N.A. 'Sandy' Mitchell, Gary Peters, Tricia Perris (GRFU), John Phillips, Redland Park United Reform Church, Ian Reed, Olly Ridge, Derek Robinson, *The Rugby Paper*, Greg Ryan, The Shaftesbury Crusade, Peter Shortell, Pamela Steadman, Sam Stride, Gilbert Tanner, Derek Thatcher, Ian Watkins, *Western Daily Press*, Andy Weymouth, John White Media.

FOREWORD

This book will appeal not just to the 'Dings Diehards' but to all those who love the game of rugby and wish to understand better the origins of our famous club. Those of us who are members of Dings Crusaders often talk of the uniqueness of the club, and it is truly so. The development of the club from its origins of necessity to where we are now, without losing the ethos, is special.

In the early days it was not just about the rugby, but about social reform and the need to provide alternatives for those families living in squalor without the benefits of today's welfare, health, social and educational provisions. The vision of men like Joseph Hinam Bell, and Revd Urijah Rees Thomas and Mr Rudge and all the benefactors who came after them, to lift the morale and wellbeing of those who lived in the Dings through social action, gave an opportunity to many to have a better life. Given the location – low lying and close to water – would have meant living in trying conditions to say the least.

As Ian traces the history of the Shaftesbury Crusade and Dings Crusaders rugby club it is not surprising that the ethos honed in those early days and still held dear in the club of always performing best when times were tough shines through. The motto, worn proudly on the club badge, *Per Crucem ad Coronam*, Through the Cross to the Crown (i.e. through suffering to victory), underlines the Christian heritage of the club.

Dings has always been a club that offers a game to all, regardless of background or circumstances, quite rightly, and this is something of which we are very proud. Over the years this has resulted in many people discovering a talent they never thought they had, good friends for life and establishing a club with its heart in the community.

Ian traces the club from its early years when it was nomadic in its playing venues, to the foresight of the club leaders in moving to Lockleaze to establish, not just a sports field, but a satellite of the Shaftesbury Crusade where the work done in the Dings area could be replicated on the newly built Lockleaze estate.

Finally, Ian points us to Frenchay and our new home, also thanks to the vision of those leading the club, and as we move forward we should never forget the past, it is the past which shapes us and in the case of the Dings it is something that makes us strong.

I thank Ian for all his hard work and passion in writing this book and I thoroughly commend it to all who love our game to read.

Revd Canon Trevor Denley
Dings Crusaders RFC

1

THE SHAFTESBURY CRUSADE

In a history of the Shaftesbury Crusade, published in 1943, there is reference to an article in an unnamed magazine published in London in the Victorian era. The article entitled 'A Glance at Clifton from Brandon Hill', after eulogising the amenities of Clifton (the middle-class suburb *par excellence*), continues as follows:

> ...furthest from the eye, a dense and almost impenetrable brown mist marks the grimy, filthy and hovel-crowded district of the Dings, where labour and squalor have shaken hand and made a compact together to withstand the opposing forces of civilisation and comfort.

The date of the article is August 1852.

The Dings, a notorious area of poverty and degradation in the St Philip's area of Bristol, between Temple Meads and Barton Hill, was one of the worst slums in the city. In this district of narrow alleys and mean houses conditions were so bad that the health of the people was impaired and ordinary comfort became impossible. The houses are described in some records as cottages, a word which has a pleasantly rural connotation, suggesting a tiny house, perhaps thatched, with roses round the door and a well-kept garden. We might use the word hovels today to describe the overcrowded, insanitary buildings clustered together in courts, sharing one outside toilet and certainly without gardens. The only place for the man of the house to get away from such uncomfortable dwellings, and squalling children, was the local public house, where there was light and warmth and companionship, but where the small family income could quickly be drunk away leaving practically nothing for their struggling wives to feed the family with. Public houses, which gave

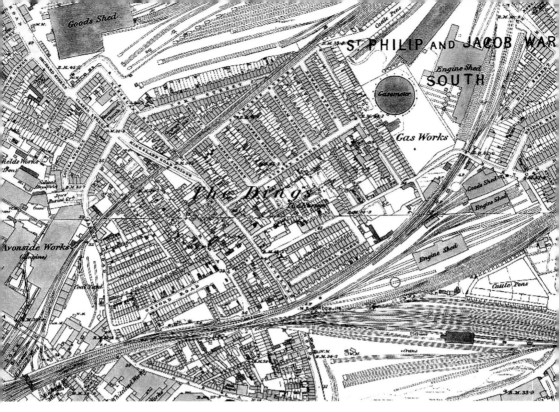

A nineteenth-century map of St Philip's, Bristol, showing The Dings area.

people the means of forgetting their wretchedness for a time, did a roaring trade, and drunkenness made bad conditions much worse.

Joseph Hinam Bell of the Cumberland Street City Mission, a young man who had been appointed by the Bristol City Mission to do pioneer Christian work in St Philip's, made a gallant attempt to deal with the alcohol problem, and largely due to Bell (a religious and social leader with such energy that he became known locally as the 'Bishop of Dings'), the St Philip's Coffee House Company was formed to provide a counter-attraction to the public houses in the area. Other prominent Christian citizens interested themselves in Bell's work and a committee was formed which proceeded to survey the district, and when the party came to the junction of Oxford Street with Kingsland Road and saw a plot of land, one of their number expressed the feelings of all when he exclaimed, 'This is the spot.' The plan was to provide a public house without intoxicating drinks, to be open from early morning till late at night, so that men going to work in the mornings might get breakfast on the way, and in the evenings might find a place of rest and recreation. The plot, previously the site of a few old cottages, was purchased in July 1885, a limited company formed with the committee becoming the first directors.

In March 1888, the Shaftesbury Workmen's Institute and Public Hall was officially opened as an alternative to the many public houses and gin

Members of the Bristol City Mission, 1900.
Joseph Hinam Bell (top centre) was a leading
figure in the creation of the Shaftesbury Hall.

palaces of the area, 'free from the taint
of intoxicants and other evil influences'.
Serving non-alcoholic drinks for the
worker, the hall opened at 5 a.m. to
serve breakfast and closed at 11 p.m.

The Revd Urijah Rees Thomas (1839–
1901), minister of Redland Park Church
from 1862 to 1901, was also aware of
the dreadful conditions in The Dings
area, and devised a scheme which he
believed had a double benefit. He saw
the needs in St Philip's and knew that
many young people in the Redland Park
Church had not sufficient outlet for their
energy and their idealism, and inquiries
were made to discover the most suitable
opening for work in the city. St Judes
and other districts were considered, but
it seemed clear to Revd Thomas that
St Philip's was the place, partly because
of the warm assurance and guidance of
Joseph Hinam Bell, and partly because
the Shaftesbury Hall stood there, by
1892 well-nigh vacant and so appealing
to be made use of. Easy terms were
made with the directors of The St Philip's
Coffee House Company and in 1893 the
Shaftesbury Mission was started in the
Shaftesbury Hall. The Revd Thomas
inspired members of Redland Park Young
People's Guild to go down to St Philip's
to run boys' and girls' clubs, sports
clubs, gymnastics classes, first aid, Bible

The Revd Urijah Rees Thomas (1839–1901),
minister of Redland Park Church from 1862 to
1901. A drinking fountain in his memory is still
resplendent on Whiteladies Road, Bristol.

Sydney Alley, located between Union Road and Kingsland Road, St Philip's, was the first venue of the Dings' Club – established by the Clifton College Mission and taken over by the Shaftesbury Crusade. (Samuel Loxton)

Founders and early officers of the Shaftesbury
Crusade. Henry Morris Harris, the son of John M.
and Louisa Harris, was president of Dings Crusaders
from 1897 to 1930.

classes and many other activities. Thus the original brigade of Shaftesbury Crusaders from Redland entered upon their life work in the St Philip's district.

The people of the area initially viewed the Mission with some suspicion and at first progress there was slow, but the objects of the new movement were explained by visitors who called on every house in the district. As the needs became known, the work quickly broadened to include people of all ages, with clubs and classes and sports teams. Gymnastics was popular, probably because it needed less space than most ball games. But the work was always centered on Christianity, and whilst not a recognised church, the Crusade held Sunday services, Bible classes and discussion groups for all ages. By 1895 Mr William Holland Harris had started the 25th Company of the Bristol Battalion of the Boys' Brigade; Mr Ernest Tribe the Men's Bible Class and the Sunday Evening Service; Mr Arthur Ernest Harris the Gymnasium. The Mission used the Shaftesbury Hall and one adjoining room, but the accommodation proved quite inadequate, for by 1898 the Girls' Club had over 160 members and the Dings' Club was conducted in Sydney Alley by Mr Henry Morris Harris because there was no room for it in the Hall.

Arthur Ernest Harris and William Holland Harris were also sons of John M. and Louisa Harris, and when their father died in 1907, he left a large sum of money for the furtherance of the Gospel Temperance Effort. By 1909 (with interest) it had reached £3,000, and was used for the new wing of the Shaftesbury Crusade, which was built in his memory.

"DINGS CYCLING CLUB. 1915."

Before the Shaftesbury Crusade was established a number of Clifton College Old Boys had founded a social club located in The Dings which gave its name to the Dings' Club for Boys and Young Men. In 1896 H.M. Harris took over the responsibility of the Club, which became part of the Crusade. A small beginning it was, amongst a few untamed youths in very dilapidated premises in nearby Sydney Alley.

In March 1898, the Coffee House Company allowed the Shaftesbury Mission to use its premises subject to payment of £25 a year rent and to liability for the mortgage of £1,500 – on condition that they extended the building. A vacant piece of land adjoining the Shaftesbury Hall afforded an excellent site for the expansion that was urgently needed, and largely due to the generosity of members of the Wills family sufficient money was raised to discharge the mortgage and pay for the ground and extensions. On 27 July 1899 the Shaftesbury Mission was incorporated under the Companies Act and became the Shaftesbury Crusade.

The new Shaftesbury building was opened and consecrated in June 1900 by Revd Urijah Thomas, the first president of the Crusade, assisted by, amongst others, Joseph Hinam Bell, the Crusade's first director. The additions included several club-rooms, a reading room and a gymnasium. The billiard room was enlarged and room for 200 additional seats was provided by an extension of the hall. Accommodation was now available for the Boys' Brigade and the popular Dings' Club, with the provision of billiards, skittles, reading, chess, draughts, dominoes, cadets, Brownies, table tennis, football, cricket, Indian clubs, brass band, male voice choir, educational classes, swimming, cycling, gymnastics, and a temperance group.

Subscription to the Dings' Club cost 1*d* (one penny) per week, payable on Saturdays, with an entrance fee of 6*d* upon joining. Every member was pledged to promote good behaviour, clean habits and right speaking in the Club – no member under 18 years of age was permitted to smoke on the Club premises. Annual subscription for membership of the rugby club was one shilling per year and rule 9 stated that, 'no one who is not a member of the Club (Dings' Club) shall play in any match'.

Opposite top The Shaftesbury Crusade Institute, built in 1900 and extended in 1909. The imposing building still stands on the junction of Oxford Street and Kingsland Road.

Opposite bottom The Dings Cycling Club photographed in 1915. Arthur E. Harris, an officer of the Dings' Club, is second from left in the front row, with a young Samuel John Stone to his left. Both served their country during the First World War.

2

EARLY YEARS

In 1897, H.W. Rudge founded and established Dings Crusaders Rugby Club as a part of the Dings' Club, one of the activities of the Shaftesbury Crusade. Herbert William Rudge, a prominent member of the Shaftesbury Crusade and the original driving force behind the rugby club, was the club's first honorary secretary, holding office for thirty years before becoming club president in 1930.

Rudge was born in the Redland area of Bristol in 1875, the son of Charles King Rudge, a physician and surgeon, and his wife Louisa Maria. The Rudge family home, Ashgrove House at No. 145 Whiteladies Road, Clifton, was an imposing three-storey Victorian property close to Redland Park Church, and Westfield Park, where for most of his time in Bristol the Revd Urijah Thomas lodged with his good friend Wilberforce Tribe, a member of Redland Park Church and one of the founder members of the Shaftesbury Crusade.

In a December 1892 team line-up of Clifton Crusaders (established in the 1880s) against Chepstow played on The Downs, Charles King Rudge is recorded as playing at wing three-quarter for the home side. By actively engaging in sport C.K. Rudge, the father of H.W. Rudge, may well have provided the inspiration for his son to introduce rugby to the Dings' Club. Indeed, the game was already a familiar sport in St Philip's, as one of the activities involving the public school boys from Clifton College and the members of the Clifton College Mission, in The Dings, was the annual rugby football match between the school and the Mission boys (who were taught to play rugby football especially for this match). Fletcher Robinson, in 1887, argued that:

perhaps the best features of this enthusiasm for Rugby football which has grown up among working men is the delight in hard exercise and

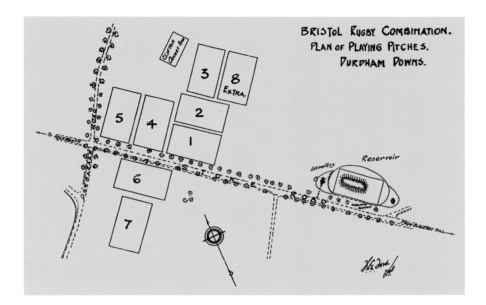

The location of the rugby pitches on Durdham Down. The section of Downleaze Road adjacent to pitch No.5 is now called Saville Road. The water tower remains a prominent feature on The Downs.

Rugby in the early twentieth century as reported by *The Illustrated Sporting and Dramatic News* features the North *v.* South match at Blackheath in January 1903.

consequent self-denial that it has taught him. A man cannot spend his nights and his wages in the public house if twice a week he has to face a hard struggle of forty minutes 'each way'.

The idea of 'a healthy body in a healthy mind' echoed much of temperance propaganda at the time and the muscular Christian belief that sport built character, held by many of the leaders of various sports, meant that these games appeared to share many of the imperatives of the temperance movement. The traditional hostility of the temperance movement – the Shaftesbury Crusade incorporated a Total Abstinence Association – to sport, at heart until the final quarter of the nineteenth century, was based largely on the fact that where there was sport, there was alcohol. However, it did come to accept that forceful methods on the football field were not inconsistent with soft drinks after the match.

By the 1890s rugby had become well established in Bristol, and in September 1890 for the purpose of governing rugby football locally ten clubs joined the Bristol & District Rugby Football Union (B&DRFU) on its formation: Bristol, Oakfield, Hornets, Clifton Crusaders (previously known as St Saviours' Club), Carlton, Knowle Church, Lodway, Vauxhall Rangers, Bristol Rangers and Portishead. By 1893 twenty-five were represented, whilst the B&DRFU list of teams for 1895 introduced twelve newcomers including Bishopston and Dings.

During this period there was a proliferation of rugby clubs in Bristol, particularly in the St Philip's area. During the 1890/91 season there is a reference in the *Bristol Mercury* newspaper to Dings Boys' Club playing against St Agnes Boys' Club Rugby Club, and by 1893/94 regular fixtures are recorded in the local press for newly founded Dings (and their Second XV) and Shaftesbury Crusaders, whilst still chronicling matches involving Dings Boys' Club (sometimes referred to as Dings Young Men's Club). The following season, 1894/95, both Dings RFC XVs are well established; the First team competing in Division 'C' of the Bristol Junior League. St Philip's Crusaders (and their Seconds) make a brief appearance that same season and then disappear from the pages of rugby history, whilst in 1895 St Philip's Rangers are listed as one of the twenty-eight members of the B&DRFU. In 1895/96 Dings First XV were members of the Bristol Rugby Union's Senior League, and by 1897 were playing regularly against sides from Bath, Cardiff, Chepstow and Frome, being referred to on occasions as Bristol Dings. Their home matches were played on a field at St Philip's Marsh called The Yearlings just across the River Avon near Sparke Evans Park, the teams changing in The Dove public house on nearby Feeder Road.

The first recorded Dings Crusaders game — taken from a handwritten contemporary fixture list — was played on 1 October 1898 against Elton St Michael's, which Dings lost 5–15; the next match, a 5–3 victory over St Mary's Seconds; the first home game, on 1 November, was a 0–0 draw with Avonmouth Seconds. Matches against Bishopston Wesley Guild, Belgrave Athletic, Bath YMCA and St Agnes also featured in that first season. Playing record for 1898/99: played 23, won 12, drawn 5, lost 6, points for 172, against 58.

In 1893 the RFU had changed the existing points system when the value of a try was raised to 3 points (from 2), making it equal in value to all goals apart from those scored from a drop kick — 4 points. This evolution of the game —

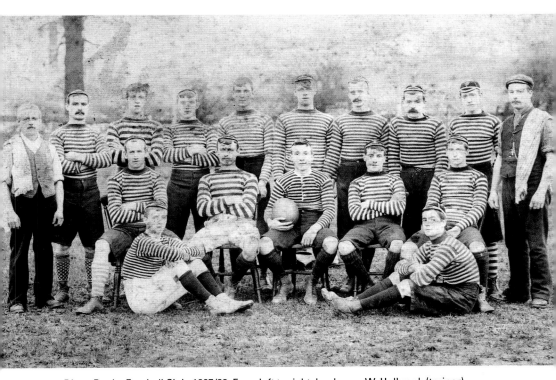

Dings Rugby Football Club, 1897/98. From left to right, back row: W. Holbrook (trainer), F. Cox, H. Towler, J. Dunn, S. Parker, E. Parker, A. Robbins, J. Gribble, Bert Weaver, J. Pinkott (trainer). Front row: Jack Brooks (vice-captain), F. Shannon, J. Hooper (captain), S. Cuff, A. Bennett. On ground: F. Bennett, W. Swainger.

which brought tries to the fore, gave rise to the passing game and started to move the sport away from its reliance on scrummaging and forward play, and the kicking of goals – was the rugby world that Dings Crusaders entered in 1898.

Early success for Dings Crusaders came in the Bristol Junior Cup final, played at St Philip's on Saturday, 20 April 1901, when they defeated St James's by 2 tries to 1 try in front of 400 spectators. According to a newspaper report of the time, 'The game produced good football, and was fought keenly from start to finish'. In the first half W. Harris crossed the line for St James's, with Berry scoring two second-half tries for Dings. 'Hallett, Berry and Hooper played splendid games for the Crusaders,' commented the *Western Daily Press*.

From the outset Dings Crusaders home games were played on The Downs, and at weekends residents of High Street in Clifton (a short, narrow road leading up to The Downs only a stone's throw from the top of Blackboy Hill) made a shilling or two by helping homeless rugby teams. For years,

Dings Crusaders teams (and their opponents) changed at a Mrs Lowe's house. The 1901 census records Ellen Lowe living at No. 38 High Street with her husband Joseph and five children. Other teams utilised nearby pubs, unthinkable for a club such as Dings Crusaders who were intrinsically associated with the Shaftesbury Crusade and their promotion of personal abstinence from alcohol, or changed in the open air. During its short-lived existence Shaftesbury RFC (their secretary was Arthur E. Harris), whose headquarters were at the Shaftesbury Institute, played on The Downs and changed in Redland Park Church Hall. St Mary's Old Boys at first had no indoor changing facilities until they made an arrangement with Mrs Kibby in the High Street. When Broad Plain began playing on The Downs in 1909 they used Mrs Dando's house to change. 'Before the game', the club's history

Dings Crusaders, Bristol Junior Cup winners 1900/01. From left to right, back row: W. Phillips, J. Rowe, A. Adams. Middle row: A. Rowe (trainer), R. Webb (vice-captain), W. Connell, W. Hallett, George Winterson, E. Matthews, James Payne. Front row: James Shortman, C. Brooks, W. Berry, Henry Hussey (captain), A. Webb, Henry M. Harris (president). On ground: E. Hooper, Frank Oatley.

DINGS CRUSADERS (Shaftesbury)—First XV. Division II.					DINGS CRUSADERS (Shaftesbury)—Second XV. Division III.			

DATE	OPPONENTS.		PLAYED	RESULT For Agnst.	DATE	OPPONENTS.	PLAYED	RESULT For Agnst.
1901					1901			
Sept. 21	Horfield	..	home		Sept. 21			
,, 28	Keynsham	..	home		,, 28	St. Agnes 3rd ..	c away	
Oct. 5	St. Agnes 2nd	c	home		Oct. 5			
,, 12	Coombe Down (Bath)..		away		,, 12	Redland ..	home	
,, 19	St. James	c	away		,, 19	Mer'hnt Venturers T.C	home	
,, 26	Long Ashton..	..	away		,, 26	Fairfield Road O.B. ..	home	
Nov. 2	Horfield	c	away		Nov. 2			
,, 9	Saracens 2nd..	c	home		,, 9	St. Agnes 3rd ..	away	
,, 16	Eversley 2nd..	c	home		,, 16	Brookland ..	c home	
,, 23	Oldfield Park (Bath) ..		away		,, 23	Brighton House Sch. c	home	
,, 30	Cotham ..	c	home		,, 30			
Dec. 7	Elton St. Michael's	c	away		Dec. 7	Ashley Down ..	c home	
,, 14	Keynsham ..	..	away		,, 14	Brighton House Sch. c	away	
,, 21	Eversley 2nd	c	away		,, 21			
,, 28	Clifton 2nd ..	..	home		,, 28	Redland ..	.. away	
1902					1902			
Jan. 4	Cotham ..	c	away		Jan. 4			
,, 11	Dings 2nd ..		away		,, 11	Fairfield Road O.B. c	home	
,, 18	Horfield ..		home		,, 18			
,, 25	Oldfield Park	..	home		,, 25			
Feb. 1	Elton St. Michael's	..	home		Feb. 1			
,, 8	Coombe Down		home		,, 8	Mer'hnt Venturers T.C.	away	
,, 15	Long Ashton..	..	home		,, 15	Ashley Down ..	c away	
,, 22	Dings 2nd ..	c	home		,, 22	St. Agnes 3rd	c home	
Mar. 1	Clifton 2nd ..	..	away		Mar. 1	Brookland ..	c away	
,, 8	St. James ..	..	away		,, 8			
,, 15	Saracens 2nd	c	away		,, 15	Brookland ..	.. home	
,, 22	St. Agnes 2nd	c	away		,, 22	Fairfield Road O.B. c	away	
,, 29					,, 29	St. Agnes 3rd ..	home	
Apr. 5					Apr. 5			

Hon. Sec.—H. W. Rudge, 145, Whiteladies Road.
Colours—Blue and White Hoops.
Dressing Room—Mrs. Lowe, High St., Clifton.
Ground—Downs.

Hon. Sec.—
Colours—Blue and White Hoops.
Dressing Room—Mrs. Lowe, High St., Clifton.
Ground—Downs.

Fixtures for Dings Crusaders First and Second teams as they appeared in the Bristol Combination handbook of 1901/02. The letter 'c' denotes a 'competitive' league game.

states, 'the poles and flags had to be collected from Mr Lowe's yard in the High Street, carried on to The Downs and fixed up. After the game poles and flags were brought back to Mr Lowe's yard, then a wash in one galvanized bath. First there got a bath, the remainder – not so good.'

Despite its popularity in the South West, in Bristol the game found itself fighting for its life against the soccer tidal wave. In 1900, the Bristol & District Rugby Football Union told the RFU that it was 'being killed' by the round ball game and that if league competitions were not allowed, 'the younger portion of players would go over to the association code'. Consequently, the Bristol & District Rugby Football Combination league competition was established – against the wishes of the RFU – in the summer of 1901 partly in response to the growing popularity of soccer in the city, but also for the promotion of Rugby Union Football and to provide a focus for the large number of clubs in the area and the mutual wellbeing of those clubs. These clubs ranged from Avonmouth, a side composed largely of dockers, to Old Colstonians, made up of ex-pupils of Colston's School, a private school in Bristol.

In the Bristol Combination's inaugural season (1901/02) Dings finished top of Division I, winning the Championship Cup, with Dings Crusaders

First and Second XV's winning Divisions II and III respectively. The clubs competing in the Combination's inaugural season, with their finishing positions, were:

Division I	Division II	Division III
Dings	Dings Crusaders	Dings Crusaders II
Bristol North	Dings II	Fairfield Old Boys
Knowle	Horfield	Brookland
Stapleton Road	Elton St Michael's	Brighton House School
Saracens	Eversley II	St Agnes III
Eversley	Cotham	Ashley Down Old Boys
St Agnes	Saracens	
	St Agnes II	

The new Bristol Combination proved exceedingly popular in its first season, and at the end of the season there was a gathering of over 100 local rugby men at the Montague Hotel in Kingsdown Parade; the purpose of which was to present the three cups to the leaders in the three divisions. The chairman referred to the good local rugby had derived from the competitions, and said 'The Dings were the leaders in Division I, the Dings Crusaders Division II, and the Dings Crusaders Reserves were first in the 3rd Division', and he thought 'there was a great Dings' flavour about this, but the respective champions certainly deserved their honours.'

Traditionally during that era, at the start of a new season the winners of the previous season's division played against a team representative of the rest of the clubs forming the division. Therefore, on Saturday, 13 September 1902, on the Saracens' ground at Ashley Down, Dings Crusaders,

Bert Weaver, secretary of Dings RFC in the early 1900s and honorary treasurer of the Bristol Combination in its early years, played for Dings RFC in the 1890s.

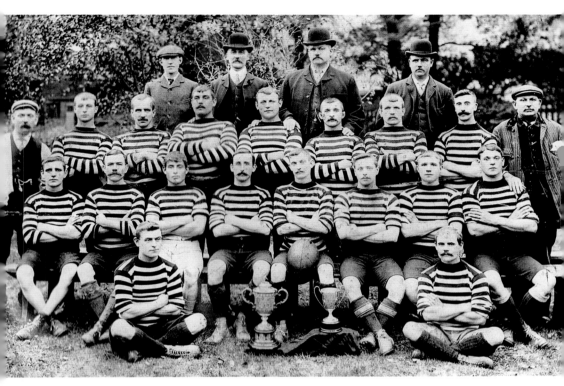

Dings Rugby Football Club, 1904/05, winners of the Gloucestershire Junior Cup and Bristol Combination Cup (1st Division). From left to right, back row: Bert Weaver (secretary), T. Harvey (committee), R. Hall (committee), G. Parker (treasurer). Middle row: H. McDowell (trainer), W. Tomlin, A. Jones, S. Parker, F. Shannon (vice-captain), W. Ryan, W. Berry, E. Hobbs, -?-. Front row: Thomas Witcombe, G. Hill, J. Smith, A. Llewellin, E. Woolner, Herbert James Tadd, Henry Bessell, S. Bessell. On ground: H. Mough, H.J. Price.

champions of the Second Division of the Bristol Rugby Combination, played the 'Rest of the Combination'. Dings' line-up for the game was: Hennessy, back; Naylor, Hussey (captain), Equall and Brooks, three-quarters; Oatley and Hooper, half-backs; Mayer, J. Phillips, Rowe, Webb, Fowler, Shortman, Smart and Adams, forwards. Referee: Mr J.J. Ford. Alderman Harry Hennessy, one of Dings Crusaders' early players, became chairman of Bristol City Council and various committees.

The *Western Daily Press* reported the match:

Crusaders won the toss, and elected to play downhill, the Combination having the wind and sun in their faces. The Crusaders started by pressing the Combination team back, and Brooks, of the Crusaders, made a good run, and nearly scored, the Crusaders pressing and their halves getting ball out repeatedly. After a scrum close to the line, Equall, of the Crusaders, scored a try, and converted it into a goal. From a scrum near the Combination line, Naylor made mark, but was not successful with the kick. Half-time score: Dings Crusaders, 1 goal; Combination, nil. The second half started with the Combination pressing, and Babbington of the Saracens nearly scored in the corner. The play of the Combination improved after a bit, but about five minutes from time one of the St Michael's players got hurt, and was led off the field, the Combination playing one man short for the rest the game. The Crusaders pressed, and just after some nice passing along the line nearly ended in Crusaders scoring. The game ended the Crusaders winning 1 goal to nil. Result: Crusaders, 1 goal; Combination, nil.

The following season (1902/03) Dings Crusaders Second XV continued their success by finishing top of Division III once again, winning the Cup ahead of St Agnes Thirds, whilst Dings Crusaders First team finished as runners-up to Horfield in Division II. In what appears to have been a lively First XV match against Combe Down on The Downs, the *Bath Chronicle* reported, 'One or two occasions a bitter spirit was manifested, and once a fight seemed inevitable between a Bristolian and a Downite. The offenders, however, were promptly reminded of their folly, and were called to order by the referee.' Another keenly fought match must have taken place on 28 March 1903 on The Downs when Dings Crusaders First XV defeated their Second team by 15 points to 7.

In 1904/05 Dings RFC won the Division I Cup and retained it the following season, and were also triumphant in the Gloucestershire Junior Cup final. The same season also saw Shaftesbury RFC, in only their second season, win the Division II Cup. Based at the Shaftesbury Institute in Kingsland Road the team played on The Downs, using Redland Park Church Hall as their dressing rooms, and were considered to be good enough by the Bristol Combination to be promoted to Division I the following season. A new club, St Philip's, took Shaftesbury's place in Division II. Dings RFC lifted another trophy in March 1907 when they defeated Stapleton Road in the Gloucestershire Junior Cup Final by 1 penalty goal to nil, Garrod kicking the winning points.

During this period rugby was flourishing 'down the Dings' with at least three separate clubs in existence, two directly associated with the Shaftesbury Crusade, whilst Dings RFC, another club in the St Philip's area, having no apparent affinity to the Christian mission. However, sometime between 1908 and 1910 both Dings and Shaftesbury rugby clubs ceased to exist. All three – Dings, Dings Crusaders, and Shaftesbury – were active in 1907/08, but it appears that by the following season Dings RFC had retired from competition and were no longer playing matches: whilst the 1909/10 season saw the demise

Shaftesbury RFC First XV, Bristol Combination Cup winners (Division II), 1904/05. From left to right, back row: F. Mayes, Harry Hennessey, Maurice Connell. Middle row: F. Vowles (trainer), H. Towler, James Payne, F. Smart, R. Webb, A. Mayes, A. Adams. Front row: F. Brookman (trainer), A. Webb, W. Dwyer, Henry Hussey (captain), James Shortman, Arthur E. Harris (secretary). On the ground: E. Hooper, Jack Brooks.

of Shaftesbury RFC. The reason for the disappearance of two of the 'Dings' rugby clubs and the survival of Dings Crusaders has not been established; however, it is possible that St Philip's could no longer sustain the number of players required for half-a-dozen rugby XVs, or that association football was now beginning to dominate working-class sport. Perhaps there was consolidation with a combining of the three clubs, which may be evident in the fact that in 1909/10 Dings Crusaders First XV won the Combination Second Division Cup; played 26, won 20, drawn 1, lost 5, points for 241, points against 75.

When Dings Crusaders were inaugurated in 1897 they played in blue and white hooped jerseys (the same colour and design as Dings RFC) until

Dings Crusaders (Shaftesbury) RFC First XV, Bristol Combination Cup winners (Division II), 1909/10. From left to right, back row: J. Heales, F. Poole, H. Ogborne, William Bryant, J. Cooksey. Middle row: G. Cave, J. Llewellyn, E. Parker, A. Davis, F. Rudman, Herbert William Rudge (honorary secretary), A. Johnstone. Front row: H. Johnstone, G. Stoate, J. Prideaux (captain), Edward Bowell, G. Bright. On ground: J. Hooper, A. Fisher (assistant secretary).

1903/04 when they adopted green and variously described as yellow/orange/amber jerseys. The change in jersey colour may have been initiated to avoid confusion between the two Dings teams, but at the same time Shaftesbury RFC also turned out in dark green and amber. There is no extant record indicating when Dings Crusaders changed to the now familiar blue and black strip, but certainly from 1913 onwards they have worn it.

There has been much conjecture over the years as to which Dings club James Peters, the first black man to play Rugby Union for England, played for. According to Bristol's annual report of 1900/01, James Peters joined the club from Dings Second XV, and the annual dinner of Dings Rugby Club at the Crown and Dove public house on 14 September 1901 included as one of its guests a certain J. Peters, of Bristol FC. Whilst not conclusive, it would appear from this evidence that Peters played for the longer established Dings RFC. Peters moved to Plymouth RFC in 1902 and made his England debut against Scotland on 17 March 1906.

The declaration of war on 4 August 1914 caught the RFU by surprise and it initially believed that the season should continue. But hopes of continuing the 1914/15 season rapidly melted away as players flocked to the colours. On 4 September the RFU Committee formerly cancelled all club, county and international matches, and called upon all players aged between 19 and 35 to enlist. The local rugby authority also acted quickly, for at a meeting of the Bristol & District Rugby Football Combination a fortnight later a resolution recommending that clubs with First and (or) Second teams cancel fixtures was unanimously carried. Dings Crusaders was one of the eleven clubs represented at the meeting who agreed to the proposal. Prior to that autumn evening, local rugby clubs had been preparing for the coming season with Dings Crusaders First and Second XVs looking forward to forthcoming fixtures against some familiar sides – St Mary's, Barton Hill and Avonmouth – and some not so familiar names – Anglesea, and St Nicholas with St Leonard Old Boys. However, just over a month after Britain's declaration of war all clubs were asked to cancel all of their fixtures. On the 15 September the RFU circulated a notice to all rugby clubs expressing a hope that 'all Rugby players will join some force in their own town or county'. It was time to play 'The Greater Game'.

Officers of the Shaftesbury Crusade, October 1916. Gunner H.W. Rudge is the inset photograph on the left, Arthur Ernest Harris, the artilleryman, centre. Others identified are: Ernest Tribe, Percy Steadman, Ernest James Thierry Broad, Miss Mabel Tribe, Miss Bessie L. Harris and Miss Jean Nott. Henry Morris Harris, president of Dings Crusaders, is seated far right.

3

BETWEEN THE WARS

In April 1919 the Bristol Rugby Combination resumed activities and recommenced fixtures for the 1919/20 season, although many clubs found it difficult to field teams due to a shortage of players. There were in the region of 800,000 United Kingdom military deaths during the First World War plus 1.6 million UK military wounded. Sixty-two members of the Shaftesbury Crusade lost their lives.

One individual who did survive the conflict was Gunner H.W. Rudge of the Royal Field Artillery. Herbert William Rudge, a pre-war Territorial with the 2nd South Midland Brigade, Royal Field Artillery who were based at the Artillery Grounds, Whiteladies Road, was recalled to the colours and arrived in France with his battery on 27 March 1915. Rudge survived the war and returned to carry on his work with the Shaftesbury Crusade, the Dings' Club, and as honorary secretary of Dings Crusaders RFC.

With an end to hostilities the Bristol Combination, in July 1919, began to consider how to revive rugby in Bristol. Dings Crusaders attended a meeting at the Montpelier Hotel where, together with eight other clubs, a lengthy discussion took place on the question as to whether friendly or competitive games were to be played during the coming season, and the opinion of the majority of representatives was that competitive matches should be dropped and a knock-out cup introduced.

By the 1920s Dings Crusaders were well established within the Bristol Combination, the period when a cup competition was revived – as a knock-out contest, not a system of leagues. In 1919/20 Saracens beat Bishopston in one knock-out cup semi-final, and Dings needed a replay to get past St Mary's Old Boys in the other. The first match ended in a draw of 6 points all, Budd scoring a try for Dings to equalise St Mary's penalty goal, with Cleaves then putting

The Clifton Chronicle reports the 1920 Bristol Combination Cup final between Dings Crusaders and Saracens. Dings won the match 3–0 after extra-time.

Crusaders in front. Marks then scored a try for St Mary's. The second meeting ended in a victory for Dings by 2 penalty goals to nil, Cleaves kicking the first penalty goal followed by one from Bowles. In the Combination Cup final played at Knowle in April there was no score in normal time so extra time was played, with Budd getting the winning try for the Crusaders. Cup rugby was hard – too hard, many people thought, and soon the competition was scrapped.

During this era Dings Crusaders played many traditional and familiar opponents: Avonmouth Old Boys, Bishopston, Broad Plain, Cotham Park, Imperial, Knowle, Saracens, and St Mary's Old Boys. Other teams are less well known to us today: Bristol Roundabouts, Depot Gloucestershire Regiment, GWR, Horfield Church, Ministry of Pensions, and St Luke's Church.

Just as there is confusion regarding rugby clubs with similar names and/or the same affiliations based in the St Philip's area in the late nineteenth century, in the 1920s a different conundrum existed. In the 1923/24 Bristol Combination Handbook, fixtures are listed for Dings Crusaders Old Boys' RFC First XV and Juniors, both of whom played their home matches on The Downs. The secretary was W.H. Rudge, the dressing room at the Shaftesbury Athletic Headquarters, Highland Square, High Street, Durdham

Dings Crusaders RFC First XV, Bristol Combination Senior Cup winners, 1919/20. From left to right, back row: Edmond Pavey, G. Stacey, B. Parsons, Charles Bowell, Henry Cooksey (vice-captain), J. Kelly (assistant secretary), Frederick Templar. Middle row: H.W. Rudge (honorary secretary), Maurice Connell, H. Johnstone, W.H. Budd, R. Matthews, Henry M. Harris (president). Front row: Arthur Cleaves, Sidney Wollen, William Bryant (captain), Edward Bowell, C. Daniels. On ground: J. Hooper, G.C. Osborne.

Down, and jersey colours were blue and black. By 1927/28 Dings Crusaders Old Boys' RFC and Dings Crusaders are listed separately, the 'Old Boys' with one team, 'Crusaders' with a First and Second XV. All three sides played their home games on The Downs, used the Shaftesbury Athletic Headquarters as their dressing room, and all wore blue and black jerseys.

The minute book of the Bristol Combination meeting held on 25 September 1929 recorded: 'Dings Crus. O.B. This club was stated to be wishing to change its name to Avonside RFC, running under new management…' (there was an Avonside Paper Mill and Engine Works in St Philip's). Avonside were thereupon elected to the Combination (proposed by Dings Crusaders and seconded by St Agnes). The former secretary of Dings Crusaders Old Boys, William

T. Bryant (67 William Street, Totterdown), transferred his responsibilities to the newly formed club, which initially continued to play its home games on The Downs, making use of the changing facilities at Mrs Lowe's house in High Street once more. Now resplendent in red, white and black 2-inch ringed shirts, Avonside's first season produced 11 wins from 22 matches played, with 6 defeats. For the 1933/34 season Avonside moved to the Combination's new rugby sports ground at Filton, but had ceased activities following the 1935/36 season, by which time Dings Crusaders were fielding three sides.

By 1930/31, Dings had also found a new home, or more correctly two of their sides had, when the First and Second teams, after over thirty years of playing home matches on The Downs, relocated to contest home fixtures at Henbury Hill House, the Westbury-on-Trym residence of the Steadman family. The concluding match, on 5 April, of the 1929/30 season and the last ever Dings Crusaders First XV game played on The Downs, resulted in a 17 points to 5 victory over Horfield Athletic.

Percy Steadman purchased Henbury Hill House in the early 1920s from the previous owner, Sir Thomas J. Lennard, the chairman of Lennard's Ltd. Born in 1870, the son of Henry and Harriette Steadman, Percy became a governing director of H. Steadman and Co. Ltd, the Bristol shoe firm his father founded in 1862, and subsequently a director of the boot and shoe manufacturing company founded in 1896 by the Lennard brothers. Steadman was chairman of the Shaftesbury Crusade for a quarter of a century and was a worker there from about a year after it was formed. A story told by Jack Steadman was about a fellow who was up before the 'Beak' for a minor offence. However, the fortunate individual was only given a suspended sentence

James Payne played for Dings Crusaders in the 1900/01 Junior Cup winning team and for Shaftesbury RFC in their 1904/05 Division II Cup-winning XV, before moving to Imperial. He played thirty-one games in the pack for Bristol between 1909 and 1911 and returned to Dings Crusaders in the 1920s.

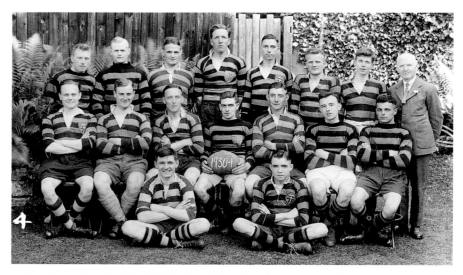

Dings Crusaders First XV, 1930/31. From left to right, back row: Les Howell, Jack Brooks, Bob Parsons, Arthur Payne, Albert Sperring, Ernest Seward, Les Robbins, H.W. Rudge (president). Front row: Jack Steadman, Jack Vaughan, Fred Payne, Albert Duffett, Tom Paul, Fred Pearce, W. Townsend. On ground: Joe Rogers, Gilbert Tanner.

Dings Crusaders Second XV, 1931/32. From left to right, back row: John Buchanan Steadman (honorary secretary), J. Coles, Gilbert Tanner, I. May, C. Munden, Charlie Hennys, A. Raymond, Thomas Oaten, H.W. Rudge (president). Front row: Leslie Seward, D. Thomas, Harry Brooks, Ivor Seward (captain), P. Welsh, Keith Steadman, W. Baker (vice-captain). Played 24, won 21, drawn 3, lost 0.

because he was due to play for the Dings on the Saturday. The magistrate was Jack's father, Percy Steadman. He died 10 August 1961, aged 90 years. Among the organisations represented at his funeral were the Dings' Club, the Shaftesbury Crusade and Dings Crusaders RFC.

Dings' First and Second teams played on the recreation ground adjacent to Percy Steadman's house at Henbury Hill House, whilst the Third team continued to play on The Downs, changing in the Shaftesbury Athletic Headquarters in Highland Square. The Henbury dressing rooms were opposite Blaise Castle entrance in 'Henbury Hill House Garage'.

Gilbert Tanner recalled the move:

After playing rugby on The Downs we were lucky to have one of the officers of the (Dings) club whose name was Steadman. He lived in Henbury Hill House with a large field and stables at the rear which he turned into a rugby field and changing rooms. We played there until the family sold the home to a girls' college.

Percy Steadman (1870–1961), a founder member and benefactor of the Shaftesbury Crusade and Dings' Club, was Sheriff of Bristol in 1917. Two sons, Percy Keith and John Buchanan Steadman, both played for Dings Crusaders, with Jack acting as honorary secretary from 1930 until 1961.

Training nights were still held in the gym at the Shaftesbury Institute on a Wednesday evening, with a run along Feeder Road as far as the Netham and back down Victoria Avenue, followed by a cold shower for everyone before they left. On Saturday nights Ernest Seward led a singsong in the club and if all three teams won, free cocoa was issued to the players. During this period there were a number of brothers who played for the club: Bill and Jim Wells; Olly and Harry Cromwell; Jack and Percy (Keith) Steadman; Ernest, Leslie, Ivor, Sidney and Dennis Seward; Jack, Bill and Harry Brooks (the celebrated front row); Tom and Jim Batten; Fred and Arthur Payne.

However, it was to be a short-lived stay at Henbury for the blue and blacks as all three Dings teams moved to the Thrissell Engineering sports ground

Henbury Hill House (beyond the tennis courts) was the Westbury-on-Trym home of the Steadman family during the 1920s and '30s. Dings Crusaders' First and Second teams played home matches here from 1930 to 1934.

in Downend for the start of the 1934/35 season. Washing facilities were in two large tin baths at the ground, and there was always a rush to get in first. The groundsman was a Mr Stone, who had played in goal for Bristol Rovers. One game that all players looked forward to was at Clifton College, where hot showers were available and a meal provided after the game. In October 1939 Dings sent two teams to play against the College's Second and Third XVs on College Close. The College Seconds were not really strong enough for Dings First XV on this occasion, and the heavier pack set up a 29 points to nil victory. Dings Second XV won by the narrow margin of 11 points to 9.

For the first time in almost twenty years Dings Crusaders added some silverware to the trophy cabinet when they won the Bristol Combination seven-a-side tournament held at the Memorial Ground in April 1937. Before the advent of the Knock-out Cup Competition, the seven-a-side tournament was the major competitive event in the Combination's calendar. In a close semi-final encounter, Dings beat St Nicholas by 5 points to nil, C. Guest scoring the only try of the game, which Joe Rogers converted. The final against Old Wickonians proved to be a hard-fought affair with Old Wickonians having the better of the first half. Three points to nil down at half-time, a penalty kicked by Joe Rogers, tries by Charlie Bowell and Albert Cooksey – both converted by Rogers – gave Crusaders a 13 points to 3 victory. In their five games in the tournament Dings scored no fewer than 61 points, with only 3 – a penalty try – recorded against them.

The final full season before the outbreak of the Second World War, 1938/39, was a remarkable campaign for the First XV, earning them the title 'The Unbeatables'. Already a formidable outfit with players such as Harry Cromwell, Tom Paul, Ern Seward, Maurice Graham, Fred Payne, Les Fynn, Bill Pell, Joe Rogers, Gilbert Tanner and Harry Brooks, the team was bolstered by the return of England international Arthur Payne. Loyalty to their club has always been an outstanding feature of the Dings Crusaders and this was particularly marked when Payne returned to his old club from Bristol to captain the team.

Gilbert Tanner's certificate for three years' service to the Dings' Club at the Shaftesbury Crusade, presented to him in September 1934. Signatories on the certificate include Jack Steadman, H.W. Rudge, Arthur E. Harris, Henry M. Harris and Arthur Henry Cork.

Dings Crusaders, 1937. From left to right, back row: -?-, E. Ball, William Brooks, Tom Paul, Nick Patten, Ken McDowell, H. Williams, Fred Payne, Albert Cooksey, Arthur Gray, Arthur Cork. Middle row: C. Guest, Maurice Graham, Charlie Bowell, B. Davage, Gilbert Tanner. Front row: Harry Brooks, Sidney Seward, Joe Rogers, Harry Cromwell, Ernest Seward.

Dings Crusaders, Bristol Combination Senior seven-a-side tournament winners, 1937. From left to right, back row: C. Guest, J. Horton, John B. Steadman (honorary secretary), Albert Cooksey, William Pell. Front row: Charlie Bowell, Harry Brooks (captain), Joe Rogers.

Dings Crusaders First XV ('The Unbeatables') 1938/39 season: played 29, won 28, drawn 1. From left to right, back row: Harry Cromwell, Tom Paul, Ernest Seward. Middle row: Jack Steadman (honorary secretary), Nick Patten, Maurice Graham, Fred Payne, K. Green, Les Fynn, William Pell, Herbert W. Rudge (president). Front row: Charlie Bowell, Ken McDowell, Joe Rogers (vice-captain), Arthur Payne (captain), Gilbert Tanner, Arthur Gray, Harry Brooks.

In the penultimate game of the season Dings defeated Portishead 22–0, and in so doing preserved their unbeaten record of 28 wins from 28 games. The final match on 1 April 1939, watched by a big crowd on the Combination Ground, was against longstanding rivals St Mary's Old Boys. The *Bristol Evening Post* reported proceedings:

The first half was of a ding-dong nature, both teams appearing afraid to open up, and play was mostly of a forward battle. In the second half, however, things vastly improved. The Old Boys went off with a rush, but Dings then became the aggressors, and St Mary's rarely got out of their own half. In the last 15 minutes it was all Dings. Green, the left-wing, had the cruel luck to be called back after a run nearly half of the field and a few minutes later he crossed the line again only to knock the flag over in touching down. On the other wing Bowell made wholehearted attempts to force his way through, and the crowd was kept on tenterhooks with St Mary's line receiving such

Dings Crusaders Second XV, 1938/39 season: played 26, won 10, drawn 2, lost 14. Points for 196, against 154.

a battering. A wonderful defence held out, however, and the final whistle went with no score. The Dings' final record is: Played 29, won 28, drawn 1, lost 0, points for 473, points against 21.

The magnificent two-year unbeaten record continued into the following season until it was final broken on 18 November 1939, when Imperial defeated Dings by 11 points to 6, Crusaders points coming from a Gilbert Tanner penalty goal and an unconverted Les Fynn try.

In October 1939 the Bristol Combination made it clear that a number of clubs would carry on playing despite difficulties of grounds in some cases and insufficient players in others, but the great majority had decided to close down following the onset of the Second World War. Dings Crusaders were one of sixteen clubs who decided to continue managing to play fifteen matches in 1939/40, but with the nation at war once more sport was a secondary consideration.

4

ARTHUR PAYNE

Throughout its history Dings Crusaders has sent a considerable number of players to the Bristol Club; some have played in the county sides and in the 1930s one player, Arthur Payne, was capped twice for his country, achieving the notable distinction of gaining a full England cap without featuring in a trial game.

Arthur Thomas Payne was born in Bristol in November 1907, the son of Francis Alfred and Ellen Payne. In 1911 the Payne family were living in Folly Lane, St Philip's, including Arthur aged 4, and his 6-year-old brother Frederick. Joining Dings Crusaders in the 1920s (his uncle James played for the club during that period), Payne began his Bristol career at the start of the 1931/32 season, appearing for the 'Whites' in the first Bristol trial match on 2 September, whilst his Dings team-mate Gilbert Tanner played at full-back for the 'Colours' against him. Arthur was selected for the Bristol United side against Abergavenny

Dings Crusaders' Arthur Payne made his two appearances for England in 1935 against Ireland and Scotland.

The England team selected to play Ireland at Twickenham on 9 February 1935. Arthur Payne (third from right in the back row), made his international debut in this match.

in early September, before making his Bristol debut against Royal Naval Engineering College in October 1931, and was awarded his First team cap at the end of that season. His career with Bristol flourished and Payne was Bristol's leading appearance maker in the 1932/33 season. Selection for Gloucestershire followed, with Payne making his county debut in October 1933 against Monmouthshire at Newport.

A regular in the county side by the following season, Payne was a member of the Gloucestershire side beaten 10–0 by East Midlands at Northampton in the English Rugby County Championship final in March 1934. He was injured in the Bristol match against Gloucester at Kingsholm on 28 September 1935, sustaining a severe strain in a thigh muscle, the result of which meant that he was unable to take his place in the Gloucestershire and Somerset Combined Counties side that lost 23–3 to the touring New Zealand All Blacks on 3 October that year at the Memorial Ground. He played for Gloucestershire in the County Championship group matches versus Devon, Somerset and Cornwall in 1936, but was injured for the semi-final against Kent at Kingsholm, his place taken in the middle of the back row by J.P. Haskins of Bristol, and he also missed the final which Gloucestershire won 5–0 versus East Midlands at the Memorial Ground in Bristol.

Arthur Payne was selected for England without appearing in a trial match, being chosen to represent his country almost entirely on his club form. He made his international debut at number 8, replacing Blackheath's Dudley Kemp in the back row, at Twickenham on 9 February 1935 against Ireland in a 14–3 victory. The *Western Daily Press* reported his performance thus:

> A.T. Payne, the only new cap in the side, gave an impressive display. Several times he was conspicuous in stopping the Irish rushes by his fearlessness in going down to the ball, whilst he executed a number of neat kicks to touch to relieve pressure. The ball seemed to evade him in the open and he rarely had the chance to open up. He was, too neglected in the line-out, the ball seldom reaching him.

In an unchanged pack, Payne was retained in the back row for the Calcutta Cup match versus Scotland on 16 March 1935 at Murrayfield. In front of 65,000 spectators Scotland regained the Cup, winning by 10 points to 7.

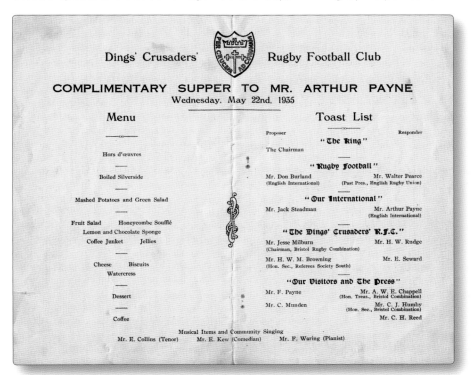

A complimentary supper was held at the Shaftesbury Crusade to celebrate Arthur Payne's selection for England. It was an alcohol-free event!

The press again reported Payne's contribution: '… while Clarke, in particular, Payne, Longland, and Weston were outstanding for England'.

To celebrate Payne's selection for the national side a complimentary supper was organised by Dings Crusaders in the Shaftesbury Institute with guests from the RFU, the Bristol Combination and Bristol RFC. But, according to Charlie Murphy, the former Bristol team-mate of Payne, 'There was no beer with the dinner. The guests were merely offered lemonade, which was available in jugs.' When the guests left the 'official' celebration they all made a beeline for the pub opposite the Shaftesbury Crusade, which did a roaring trade that night.

Renowned as a line-out specialist, his work rate and tactical kicking, Arthur Payne made 162 appearances for Bristol, his final game for the club being at Cardiff in 1937. He played fifteen times for Gloucestershire and on two occasions for England. On the completion of his Bristol career he turned out for Weston-super-Mare before returning to captain Dings for the 1938/39 season, teaming up once more with brother Fred and former Bristol team-mate Gilbert Tanner. The last season before the Second World War was a resounding success for Dings Crusaders First XV, being undefeated in 29 games (28 wins, 1 draw).

During the Second World War Payne turned out for a number of sides, including Bristol Supporters Rugby Club (a number of Bristol games were played under the guise of the supporters Club at this time), in charity and friendly matches against service teams, and he eventually did play against an 'All Blacks' side when the Revd Brooks' West of England XV played the New Zealand Expeditionary Force Rugby XV at the Memorial Ground in December 1940. Towards the end of his playing career Payne also turned out for the Bristol Gas Company and coached the B.A.C. team. An aircraft engineer at Filton, and a vice-president of Dings Old Boys' Society, Arthur Payne died on 6 June 1968, aged 60 years.

5

THE MOVE TO LOCKLEAZE

After the end of the Second World War, the Dings area was listed for industrial development and many of the houses were demolished, which relocated most of the members of the Shaftesbury Crusade. The building in Kingsland Road was closed, the leaders moving to the old Quaker school buildings in Barton Hill, but still the Crusade was to evolve.

Shortly after the construction of a new council housing estate in the Lockleaze area of Bristol, 12 acres of land were purchased at the end of Landseer Avenue in 1948 by the Lockleaze Recreation Ground Charitable Trust – a charity set up by the Shaftesbury Crusade in an effort to establish their Mission in what was then a new suburb. The Shaftesbury established a Sunday school and Boys' Brigade Company (the 50th Shaftesbury Crusade), but the establishment of a church never actually got off the ground – because a minister could not be found to run it. The move to Lockleaze – brought about primarily by Jack Steadman – provided a facility that enabled the formation of a number of groups and clubs, and the creation of a permanent home for Dings Crusaders Rugby Club, which established it at the heart of the Lockleaze community.

Ten years on from their previous triumph Dings Crusaders once again emerged victorious in the Bristol Combination Senior seven-a-side tournament held at the Memorial Ground at the end of the 1946/47 season. Having beaten Imperial 7–3 in their semi-final game, Dings, captained by Jack Harris, defeated St Mary's Old Boys in the final by 5 points to nil.

To celebrate the founding of both clubs in 1897, a Jubilee match between Dings Crusaders and Avonmouth Old Boys was played at the Memorial Ground on 14 April 1948, in what was described in the press as 'a typical battle between two Combination sides, extremely fast and keen, with

The Shaftesbury Crusade huts, Landseer Avenue, *c.* 1952. Following the development of Lockleaze, a field was acquired by the Shaftesbury Crusade, where two old army huts, taken from nearby Purdown, were erected with changing rooms and a plunge bath.

fortunes fluctuating throughout'. Avonmouth led by 6 points to 0 at half-time, but Dings improved after the interval and aided by some splendid kicking from full-back Gilbert Tanner, they began to have more of the game and R. Tucker scored a try for Gray to convert. With Jack Harris, the captain, using the touchline cleverly Dings maintained the attack and eventually Green gained an unconverted try. Final score: Avonmouth Old Boys 6, Dings Crusaders 8.

When the new ground at Lockleaze was opened for the 1948/49 season Dings Crusaders had two senior and one junior team, but the club experienced a decline in fortunes when the junior side was discontinued in 1950 and it was only with great difficulty that the senior teams kept going, as players were not forthcoming. Les Fynn was chiefly responsible for reviving the club, as club officials did not ignore the problem and went out and found youngsters who did not know the game and taught them how to play rugby. At this time, a typical example of club loyalty for which Dings is noted was personified by Jack Harris who, within five games of qualifying for a Bristol blazer, forfeited his chance of that honour by asking the Bristol Club to release him to aid his club. Dings weathered the storm to such effect that during the 1956/57 season a Third XV was launched under the care of Stan Bryant and John Waterman.

Dings Crusaders, Bristol Combination Senior seven-a-side tournament winners, 1946/47. From left to right, back row: John B. Steadman, Ken McDowell, Harry Brooks, R. Milton, Leslie Seward. Front row: W. Webb, William Pell, Jack Harris (captain), R. Caldicott, Les Fynn.

THE "SHAFTESBURY"
THE SHAFTESBURY CRUSADE INC.

SALISBURY STREET BARTON HILL BRISTOL T.N. 57353
LANDSEER AVENUE LOCKLEAZE BRISTOL T.N. 691367

Barton Hill

Lockleaze

The Shaftesbury Crusade building in Landseer Avenue, Lockleaze (lower picture) was used by the Boys' Brigade, Life Boys, Girls' Life Brigade, and for a youth club run by Mrs Boaler. A Sunday school was started, with over 100 scholars, under the leadership of Jack Harris.

From 1954 the club started to build a strong relationship with the new Lockleaze Secondary School and the local community in general, with the school providing young players for the club, with training sessions held there until new facilities were built on the club's ground. It is worth noting that Romney Avenue Junior School in Lockleaze was also playing rugby in the 1950s, providing an early introduction to the game for a generation of lads, many of whom once their playing days were over would on matchdays occupy the 'Bear Pit', the corrugated roofed area located immediately outside of Dings' clubhouse, to shout encouragement to those wearing blue and black, whilst verbally (and occasionally physically) intimidating the opposition players. The advertising hoardings on the bottom touch have also taken a battering over the years as enthusiastic Dings supporters have either urged their team on, acknowledged another home try, or shown their displeasure at the visiting team. However, its closeness to the play has provided a unique atmosphere at Landseer Avenue.

The 1950s saw a number of Dings players selected for Bristol and Bristol United. The high standard of Dings' play is evident from the players who

Romney Avenue Junior School First XV, 1955/56. From left to right, back row: -?-, -?-, -?-, George Pegler. Middle row: John Knight, -?-, -?-, David Cox, Martin Hewitt. Front row: -?-, -?-, Robert Beynon, Philip Hedges, -?-. Teacher: Mr Davies.

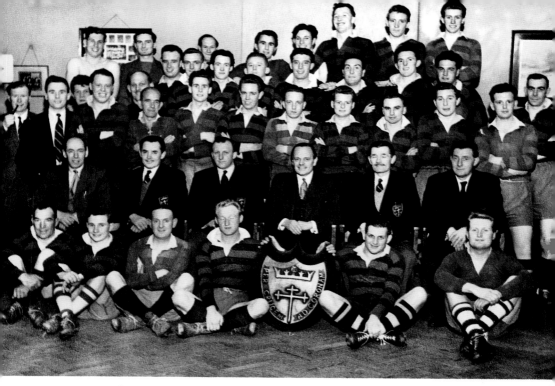

Dings Crusaders gather in the 1950s in what is believed to be one of the rooms at the Shaftesbury Crusade. Jack Steadman is seated behind the club's shield, bearing the motto *Per Crucem ad Coronam*.

The team line-ups for the Diamond Jubilee Celebration match between Dings Crusaders and Avonmouth Old Boys. Both clubs were founded in 1897.

Diamond Jubiliee Celebration Match
(1897–1957)

MEMORIAL GROUND, FILTON
(by kind permission of Bristol F.C.)

THURSDAY, 17th APRIL, 1958

K.O. 6 0 P.M.

PROGRAMME — PRICE 3d.

Dings Crusaders R.F.C. v. Avonmouth O.B. R.F.C.

DINGS CRUSADERS R.F.C.

Full Back		P. PATEMAN		
Three Quarters	R. PORTER	T. PAUL	R. CAMPBELL	R. BRIDGEMAN
Halves		G. BACKES (Capt.)	C. KIMMINS	
Forwards	D. BRINTON	A. HUDSON		G. TROOTE
		⟶ RIEMENS M. BRYANT	C. FRAMPTON	
	B. PLUMLEY	C. ALLEN		A. GRANT

AVONMOUTH O.B. R.F.C. v.

Forwards	C. SWEETLAND (Capt.)	R. EVANS		E. DAVIES
		A. MACDONALD	D. NEATE	
	J. ADAMS	P. MALE		B. LEWIS
Halves		A. STOCKEN	K. FRANKLIN	
Three Quarters	R. LISLE	H. CROOKS	K. BEAKE	M. SHAW / M. SHORE
Full Back		C. JONES		

Referee: N. WYATT (Bristol Referees Society)

Touchjudges: L. FYNN & R. GALLOWAY (Chairmen of Respective Clubs)

The Dings Crusaders side that played Avonmouth Old Boys at the Memorial Ground, 17 April 1958, in a match to celebrate both teams Diamond Jubilee season. From left to right, back row: Dave Richens, Alan Hudson, Alan Grant, Terry Paul, Ron Bridgeman. Middle row: Les Fynn (chairman), Bert Porter, George Frampton, Don Brinton, Chris Allen, Brian Plumley, Norman Wyatt (referee). Front row: Graham Troote, Bob Campbell, Grahame Backes, Colin Kimmins, Peter Pateman.

Action from the Dings Crusaders v. Avonmouth Old Boys Diamond Jubilee Celebration match played at the Memorial Ground. Dings players include Colin Kimmins, Dave Richens, Alan Hudson, Don Brinton, Bert Porter, Brian Plumley and Alan Grant. The Avonmouth player is Derek Neate.

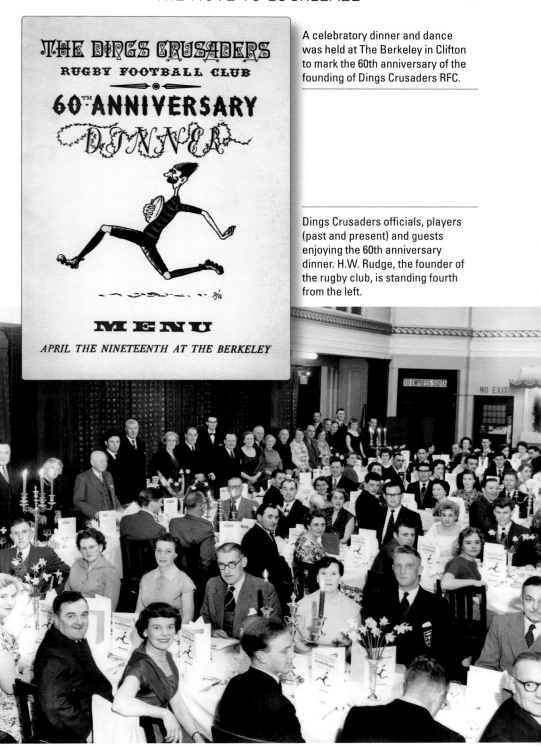

A celebratory dinner and dance was held at The Berkeley in Clifton to mark the 60th anniversary of the founding of Dings Crusaders RFC.

Dings Crusaders officials, players (past and present) and guests enjoying the 60th anniversary dinner. H.W. Rudge, the founder of the rugby club, is standing fourth from the left.

Dings Crusaders First XV, 1958/59. From left to right, back row: Terry Allen, John Troote, Graham Troote, George Frampton, Chris Allen, Colin Wallace, Alan Grant, Terry Paul, Bert Porter, Bill Pell. Front row: Trevor Hodder, Brian Plumley, Floyd Waters, Grahame Backes, Dave Williams, Tony Church.

assisted the Bristol Club during this period, namely Jack Harris, Graham Troote, Grahame Backes, Don Brinton, Ron Bridgeman, Roy Phibben, and Colin Kimmins. During his National Service, Kimmins was selected to play for East Africa against the British and Irish Lions on 27 September 1955. On the return leg of their journey from South Africa the tourists defeated East Africa by 39 points to 12 in Nairobi.

Avonmouth Old Boys and Dings Crusaders met in a Diamond Jubilee match at the Memorial Ground on 17 April 1958 to celebrate their sixty years. Dings took the lead after five minutes' play with an Alan Hudson penalty goal, Avonmouth responding with a converted try. Don Brinton then scored from a Graham Troote pass and Bert Porter converted. Avonmouth's Derek Neate scored a try which was converted, giving the Old Boys a 10 points to 8 margin at half-time, then extended their lead with another converted try. Colin Kimmins scored a second Dings try, and with the score at 15–11 it was anybody's game. Bert Porter scored a try following a strong Ron Bridgeman run, and as the game was ending in semi-darkness Crooks went over in the corner for another Avonmouth try to give them the victory by 18 points to 14.

The Diamond Jubilee dinner and dance, held at the Berkeley, Clifton in 1958 to celebrate sixty years of the club was also deemed to be a tribute to the 83-year-old H.W. Rudge who founded and established Dings Crusaders RFC as a part of the Dings' Club.

As the work of the Shaftesbury Crusade expanded at Lockleaze so that the one hut proved to be totally inadequate, a hall and extra rooms were imperative. Consequently, in 1960 an appeal went out for funds and over the next two years Redland Park members found many ways of raising money, which was concluded in a big gift day, when the Revd Norman Voice, Warden of Shaftesbury, received monetary gifts at Redland Park Church.

On 16 June 1962, a crowd converged on Lockleaze to take part in the opening of the new buildings by the Lord Mayor and Lady Mayoress. They

The Lord Mayor of Bristol, Alderman L.K. Stevenson, inspects members of the Boys' Brigade (50th Company) in Landseer Avenue on the occasion of the opening of the refurbished Shaftesbury Crusade hall, Saturday, 16 June 1962. From left to right: -?-, Dennis Sanigar, Christopher Morgan, Brian Winter, Bernard Frampton, David Ford, Leslie Sanigar, David Wildblood, Maurice Cove, Geoffrey Endicott, -?-, Alan Bryant, David Lloyd. Captain Joe Stokes accompanies the Lord Mayor, with Jack Steadman behind.

Action from a home game in the 1950s, with Lockleaze Secondary School in the background, by which time many pupils had begun a lifetime association with Dings Crusaders.

were shown a spacious hall, a well-equipped new kitchen and other rooms. The original huts and plunge bath had been completely redecorated by members of the Boys' Brigade and the opening was followed by rugger and soccer matches. Further improvements were made to the ground two years later when a new stand was constructed.

In the 1960s Les Fynn (known to many as 'Mr Dings'), a long-time supporter of the Shaftesbury and the rugby section, decided to organise a sportsmen's service at Lockleaze on a Sunday evening, persuading Trevor Denley to read at the service. He invited Peter Knight (later Reverend Peter Knight) as the preacher, who was studying at St Luke's in Exeter and played at full-back for Bristol and later England. This was in the days before the M5 motorway, and Les in his Renault drove to Exeter, picked Peter up, then drove to Bristol, before reversing the journey after the service – then he went to work on the Monday morning. This kind of dedication and commitment went above and beyond, which typifies the Dings' spirit.

On 31 August 1964, a match was organised against a team representing the Bristol club to celebrate the opening of the new Steadman Stand at Landseer Avenue, and Dings gave the Bristol XV a much closer game than the score of 19 points to 6 in favour of Bristol suggests. Named after Jack Steadman, the stand was constructed by the voluntary efforts of the rugby club members as a tribute to Steadman who served Dings Crusaders for many years, first as a player, then secretary, and finally as president. The thirty-seater stand provided an excellent view of the First XV pitch and at the time was a unique facility in the Combination.

For the first time in fourteen years Dings Crusaders picked up a trophy when they defeated Horfield Athletic in the 1960/61 Bristol Combination Senior seven-a-side tournament, a competition they had previously won in 1947. Having beaten Old Redcliffians by 11 points to 3 in the semi-final, the fresher Crusaders won the final at a canter 19–0 with tries from Edmunds, Backes and Phibben.

The playing records for this period show that Dings were maintaining their high standards of play despite the blooding of junior players into the senior team. By the 1960s the link with Lockleaze School was well established and there was no lack of young talent being brought on by the sports masters at the school, among whom were two members of the First XV, Terry Allen and John Adams. The influx of these younger players meant the

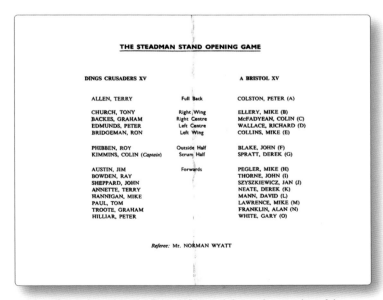

THE STEADMAN STAND OPENING GAME

DINGS CRUSADERS XV		A BRISTOL XV
ALLEN, TERRY	Full Back	COLSTON, PETER (A)
CHURCH, TONY	Right Wing	ELLERY, MIKE (B)
BACKES, GRAHAM	Right Centre	McFADYEAN, COLIN (C)
EDMUNDS, PETER	Left Centre	WALLACE, RICHARD (D)
BRIDGEMAN, RON	Left Wing	COLLINS, MIKE (E)
PHIBBEN, ROY	Outside Half	BLAKE, JOHN (F)
KIMMINS, COLIN (Captain)	Scrum Half	SPRATT, DEREK (G)
AUSTIN, JIM	Forwards	PEGLER, MIKE (H)
BOWDEN, RAY		THORNE, JOHN (I)
SHEPPARD, JOHN		SZYSZKIEWICZ, JAN (J)
ANNETTE, TERRY		NEATE, DEREK (K)
HANNIGAN, MIKE		MANN, DAVID (L)
PAUL, TOM		LAWRENCE, MIKE (M)
TROOTE, GRAHAM		FRANKLIN, ALAN (N)
HILLIAR, PETER		WHITE, GARY (O)

Referee: Mr. NORMAN WYATT

Dings Crusaders played a Bristol XV to celebrate the opening of the new Steadman Stand at the Shaftesbury Crusade sports field, as the Landseer Avenue ground was known.

The Dings Crusaders and Bristol XV teams prior to the game played on 31 August 1964.

Dings Crusaders, Bristol Combination Senior seven-a-side tournament winners, 1960/61.
From left to right: Roy Phibben (captain), Graham Troote, Floyd Waters, Peter Edmunds,
John Sheppard, Grahame Backes, Alan Hudson.

Dings Crusaders, Bristol Combination Senior seven-a-side tournament runners-up, 1962/63. From left to right, back row: Joe Rogers, Floyd Waters, Graham Troote, Grahame Backes. Front row: Ray Bowden, Peter Edmunds, Roy Phibben, Colin Kimmins, Jim Austin.

demotion of still good but older players, but, being good Dings club men, they helped the lads in the lower teams with their experience and example.

In 1968 Dings entered three teams in the Keynsham Sevens Tournament and it is was the 'A' team which progressed to the final, defeating Old Bristolians, St Brendan's 'B', Old Redcliffians and Bath University, before defeating St Brendan's 'A' 9–8 in the final courtesy of a last-minute Roy Phibben try.

Dings Crusaders First XV, *c.* 1966. From left to right, back row: John Sheppard, Martin Carter, Jim Austin, Tom Paul, Richard Potts, Richard Hook, Roy Phibben, Graham Troote, Les Fynn, Phil Knowles. Front row: Roger Bowden, Pat Clark, Peter Edmunds, Colin Kimmins, Ray Bowden, Gerry Williams.

Dings Crusaders Second XV, 1967/68. From left to right, back row: Pat Clark, Dave White, John Grinter, Mike Hannigan, Bob Sage, Brian Evans, Chris Bailey, Les Fynn (chairman). Front row: Tony Isaac, Glen Davis, Brian Plumley, Brian Winter (captain), Bob Campbell, John Phillips, Jim Challenger.

6

COME ON
YOU DINGS BOYS!

Rugby Union, with its deeply engrained culture of copious beer drinking in the clubhouse, was somewhat at odds with the temperance principles of the Shaftesbury Crusade. Indeed, Bill Winters recounted a story when the First XV were expelled by Harry Rudge for going into a pub in the 1920s, and the Second team had to fulfil the season's remaining fixtures. The after-match 'session' with its emphasis on the number of pints which could be drunk, together with the subsequent tales of copious consumption, was a vital aspect of the Rugby Union experience. However, as part of the Shaftesbury Crusade with its principle of total abstinence, this was not the case in the Dings' clubhouse as the consumption of alcohol was not permitted until 1975, when the first licensed bar was established. Prior to that, if you asked for a strong drink at Dings all you got was an extra teabag! Before 1975 the only time alcohol was allowed at the ground was for the annual Boxing Day match against Ashley Down Old Boys, when Bill Brooks would put a tot of rum in the cups of tea. These games took place whatever the weather and even after a heavy snow fall the lines were cleared to allow the match to take place.

In the 1970s the *Bristol Evening Post* first published a Merit Table based upon the results of First team games – including cup matches – between local clubs. There was no formal structure and the Bristol Combination committee initially frowned upon the idea but the printing of the tables in the newspaper was a source of great interest to players and most in the clubs. The award of the *Green 'Un* Merit Table pennant was the highlight of the season and these can still be seen adorning local clubhouses today. Consistent Dings were never out of the top five in the first eight years of Merit Table competition.

Cup competitions and leagues had very much been a feature of the Bristol Combination history prior to the First World War, but had died out in the

Dings Crusaders Third XV, 1969/70. From left to right, back row: Tony Church, Steve Bull, Brian Winter, Derek Slater, John Whittaker, Mike Hannigan, Bob Campbell, Brian Plumley, Tony Parsons. Front row: Steve Fish, Tom Kilbane, Grahame Backes (chairman), Alan Searle, John Grinter, Pete Jones.

Dings Crusaders, Gloucestershire County Cup finalists, 1972/73. From left to right, back row: John Phillips, Gerry Williams, Dave Lloyd, Derek Gunningham, Bob Williams, Richard Grant, Alan Ferris, John Thorne, Tony Watkins, Martin Carter, Phil Henson, Trevor Denley, Bob Dark. Front row: Jim Austin, Paul Lloyd, Richard Hook, Phil Knowles, John Sheppard, Pat Clark.

Dings Crusaders, Bristol Combination Knock-Out Cup winners, 1973/74. From left to right, back row: Richard Grant, Steve Butcher, Gerald Williams, Peter Mitchell, Phil Knowles, Paul Lloyd, Bob Dark, Alan Ferris, Derek Gunningham, Pat Clark. Front row: John Thorne, Bob Williams, Floyd Waters (honorary secretary), Jack Steadman (president), Richard Hook (captain), Grahame Backes (chairman), Phil Henson, Geoff Darby, Sam Stride.

1920s because of over-robust play! In 1970 the cup competition in the guise of the Charles Saunders Combination Cup was revived as the need for a more competitive edge to rugby became apparent, and this competition became a key part of the rugby calendar in the Bristol area. The final played at the Memorial Ground at the beginning of May provides a centrepiece for the Combination at the end of each season and the event attracts a large crowd of both supporters and those interested in local rugby.

Perhaps it was the prospect of being able to have a beer or two at the clubhouse which provided an incentive for the players, for in 1974 Dings won their first major silverware since 1920 when they defeated Old Redcliffians 15–13 in the final of the Bristol & District Knock-Out Cup, thanks to a Gerald Williams conversion in the sixth minute of injury time taken from in front of the posts, which just skimmed the crossbar as it went over. The previous season (1972/73) Dings Crusaders were the Bristol Combination's first representative in a Gloucestershire County Cup final, but finished as runners-up when defeated 23–0 by Clifton at Eastfield Road.

After defeating Cinderford (7–3) and Gordon League (11–9) in the earlier rounds of the 1977/78 competition, Dings were beaten 4–9 by Lydney in the semi-final of the Gloucestershire County Cup. In 1978/79 Dings Crusaders Fourth XV became the first team in the club's history to complete a season

Paul Lloyd, Richard Hook, Richard Grant and John Thorne await a throw-in during one of the traditional Boxing Day matches against Ashley Down Old Boys.

with a 100 per cent record, winning all 29 games played. The final 24–4 victory over Bristol Aeroplane Company was the 29th of the season with 918 points scored and 151 against, and this remarkable run was achieved despite the fact that over sixty players appeared for the side.

As the decade started, Dings finished top of the *Evening Post* Merit Table in 1979/80 for the first time in its history, winning 24 games of the 29 played, with just one defeat. The championship was clinched when Sammy Stride's last-minute penalty beat closest rivals North Bristol 19–18. The previous season Dings had finished in second place in the Merit Table and had built on that foundation, blending younger players into an experienced side. In 1980/81 they finished as runners-up to St Mary's in the competition. The improvement at this time was primarily due to the club's decision to make training compulsory for players. However, it wasn't necessarily the First team who were making all the headlines as, in January 1981, 16-year-old Neil Milsom scored 46 points as Dings Fourths crushed Cotham Park Fourths 114–0. Milsom, a full–back who had played for Bristol United, went over for 3 tries himself and converted 17 of the 20 tries that Dings scored.

The annual dinner in March 1980 introduced the award of caps to Dings players in recognition of the number of appearances made for the club – 300 First team games or 500 appearances in total. This was later changed to 300 club games and subsequently caps were awarded for 250 club games.

The building of potentially successful Dings sides throughout the club was starting to produce results, as in 1984 the club reached a Combination Senior Sevens final for the first time in twenty-odd years but were beaten by St Mary's Old Boys. There was now a change in the players representing the club and with the make-up of the teams. Increasingly it was lads from the Lockleaze estate or school that were wearing the royal blue and black hoops. Most of the old Shaftesbury stalwarts at Lockleaze had gone; Jack Steadman, H.W. Rudge, Arthur Payne and Les Fynn had all passed away, and as a result the rugby club took on more and more responsibility. By the early 1990s the Shaftesbury Crusade's congregation in Bristol had dwindled and in 1991 the custody of their Lockleaze site passed to the rugby club with the appointment of new trustees: Floyd Waters (president), Grahame Backes (vice-president) and Ray Bowden (chairman of selectors).

In the 1986 Combination Cup competition St Mary's Old Boys were beaten 19–5 in a close semi-final; that victory was followed by a 16–12 win over Cleve in the final, most notable for the dismissal from the field of play of a Cleve forward, the first player to be sent off in a Combination Cup final. In an

Dings Crusaders Veterans, 1976. From left to right, back row: Tony Mountford, Dennis Marshman, Brian Winter, Bill Bransome, Gordon Brown, Tony Bush, Chris Butcher, John Knight, John Phillips, Bert Angell (referee). Front row: Barry Thomas, Grahame Backes, Graham Troote, Colin Kimmins, Floyd Waters, Jim Challenger.

Dings Crusaders entertain Clevedon at Landseer Avenue. Lockleaze Secondary School in the distance, which provided many players for the rugby club, closed in 2004.

ill-tempered game, Chris Allen scored the winning try for Dings following a quickly taken tapped penalty and chip ahead by Kevin Spencer. Four members of the team – Derek Gunningham, Gerald Williams, Paul Lloyd and Richard Grant – played on the last occasion Dings won the trophy twelve years before. Phil Henson only missed the first final because of injury – testimony to the loyalty that Dings' players have for their club.

The First team finished third overall in the Merit Table in the 1985/86 season, winning 22 of their 27 games, but it was the overall strength of the club that impressed. Joint statistics for the four senior sides showed 106 wins, 4 draws and only 11 defeats in total, with a grand total of 2,694 points scored and 684 against. The First XV, who clinched the Combination Cup, had 30 wins, 4 draws and 4 defeats, but the real stars were the Fourth XV who achieved 24 victories in 25 matches and scored 789 points with 139 against. The following season the senior side again finished third in the Merit Table behind winners Avonmouth, and St Mary's Old Boys.

Dings junior sides were resurrected in 1985 following a short lapse and very quickly, with over 100 players aged from 6 to 16, rivalled in membership the senior section.

Dings Crusaders First XV, 1984/85. From left to right, back row: Noel Beresford, Chris Allen, Chris Lloyd, Richard Grant, Gary Peters, Nigel Weston, Derek Gunningham, Alan Ferris. Middle row: Phil Knowles, Gerald Williams, Steve Butcher (captain), Bob Williams, Steve Lloyd. Front row: Paul Green, Rob Stevens, Kevin Davies, Phil Henson.

Dings Crusaders v. Cleve in the 1986 Combination Cup final played at the Memorial Ground. The match was won by Dings 16–12.

Dings Crusaders, Combination Cup winners 1985/86. From left to right, back row: Derek Gunningham, Richard Grant, Paul Lloyd, Ian Westaway, Gary Peters, Jim Appleton. Middle row: Nigel Kent (touch judge), Alan Coles, Barry Grist, Derek Jones, Chris Lloyd, Nick Marment, Dave Appleton, Bob Beynon, Floyd Waters, Ian Woodgate (touch judge). Front row: Ashley Reay (referee), John Thorne, Kevin Davies, Phil Henson, Gerald Williams, Rob Stevens (captain), Kevin Spencer, Steve Lloyd, Chris Allen, Errol McKenzie.

New floodlights being installed at the Shaftesbury Crusade sport field in 1984, with all due regard to health and safety! Constructed as a memorial to Jack Steadman, who died in 1982, the lights were switched on for the first time by his widow Mabel. Jack had served Dings Crusaders as a player, administrator and president for over fifty years.

The Oggy Man

For many years a Michelin Man, a metre-high symbol of the Michelin tyre company that used to sit on top of commercial vehicles as a mascot, had proudly sat in Avonmouth Old Boys' clubhouse, painted in the red and black colours of the club with 'Avonmouth OB RFC' emblazoned across his middle. At some time during the early 1980s 'Bibendum' (his French name) mysteriously disappeared following a home game with Dings Crusaders, only to reappear at Lockleaze and take up residence there. The Oggy Man, as he is known in rugby circles, soon changed hue and was painted in the royal blue and black of Dings, much to the annoyance of Avonmouth, who requested his return. Dings politely refused the request, but added that 'You can play us for him' – and a tradition was born. Subsequently, on every occasion that Avonmouth and Dings First teams meet, the ownership of the Oggy Man is at stake together with the colour of his attire.

In the early years 'Oggy' changed hands quite often but, with the onset of league rugby, the games between the clubs became less frequent. Dings did hold on to him for about fifteen years at one time, during which time he sat behind the bar at Landseer Avenue, and was subject to many feeble attempts by Avonmouth to 'steal' him back. The Oggy Man is a fine tradition that every rugby club would love to have and creates a massive amount of interest, and players from yonder year still talk of the day they won or lost the Oggy Man. Dings Crusaders and Avonmouth Old Boys are very fortunate to have built the tradition of the Oggy Man. Whoever the 'owners' are, it creates tremendous banter and adds a certain degree of extra passion to any Dings v. Avonmouth game.

The Oggy Man resplendent in his royal blue and black hoops proudly sits in Dings
Crusaders' clubroom at Landseer Avenue, Lockleaze.

7

LEAGUE SUCCESS

Traditionally, for most of English Rugby Union's history there had been no organised leagues involving promotion and relegation, as these were seen as a sign of professionalism. The Bristol Combination had introduced leagues in 1901 but the team that finished top of their league were awarded a trophy and deemed to be Cup winners, rather than league champions. However, in the 1970s the RFU allowed the creation of regional merit leagues and a further change in attitudes towards competitiveness and money in the 1980s was reflected in the RFU's embrace not only of open commercialism but also the introduction in 1987 of a full league structure for the game. Sponsored by the brewers Courage, the new formation organised over 1,000 teams in 108 divisions, each with promotion and relegation between them.

With the league system about to become a reality, Dings Crusaders, together with other local sides, attended a number of meetings to put forward a proposal that, based on the strength of local Bristol rugby, it would be in all interests to form a Bristol-based league. Dings made the decision (believing that other clubs were doing the same) to wait and see what the RFU judgement would be and delayed replying to a Gloucestershire RFU questionnaire designed to gauge support for the leagues, feeling it would be better to wait for the Bristol Combination extraordinary meeting on the subject. Unfortunately, the South and South West league format was decided prior to that meeting taking place and, based on information from those clubs who did respond, Dings and the others who deferred were therefore accommodated at lower levels, with the Crusaders finding themselves not quite at the bottom of the league system but placed in Gloucestershire League I.

Despite the disappointment of starting the new era of rugby in Gloucestershire League I, Dings proceeded to demonstrate to those who had put the club in a lower division the folly of that judgement. Showing themselves to be one of the most consistent sides locally, in successive seasons (1987/88 and 1988/89) they topped the *Bristol Evening Post* Merit Table, winning a champions' pennant for a second and third time. During the 1987/88 season Dings suffered only one defeat against Combination teams (a 12–13 reversal against Keynsham in the Combination Cup semi-final), with the most significant victory in January when they beat Avonmouth Old Boys, the Merit Table champions for the previous three years. The 13 points to 3 defeat of the Old Boys' ended a forty-match unbeaten run against local opposition that began in December 1985. A Dings record of played 21, won 19, drawn 1, lost 1, points for 385, against 127, was sufficient to take the Merit Table champion's crown from Avonmouth.

In the inaugural Courage League season (1987/88) it was a similar playing record with just one defeat in ten games (each team was only played once), 13–22 away to Gloucester Spartans in the opening fixture. Widden Old Boys, Bream, Saracens, Cheltenham North, Drybrook, Longlevens, Old Colstonians, St Mary's Old Boys and Old Patesians were all beaten as Dings finished the season in second position behind Spartans, missing out on promotion on points difference. Progress in both cup competitions was a further achievement for the club, eventually losing to Matson 12–15 in the Gloucestershire Cup quarter-final, and reaching the semi-final of the Combination Cup to be defeated 12–13 by Keynsham, demonstrating their strength in depth by using many players in Merit Table games who weren't fielded in League matches. (The club relying to a large extent on a nucleus of long-serving forwards together with promising younger players.)

Whether or not the players adjusted sufficiently to competitive league rugby with its change in emphasis to winning the match rather than simply 'playing the game', but Dings found themselves in trouble with the rugby authorities when they were hauled before the Gloucestershire RFU disciplinary committee. The concern was with Dings' disciplinary record during 1987/88, and the committee warned Dings' officials about conduct in the club after five players were sent off within the year. There had been four dismissals the previous year. There had also been an unfortunate incident during a match with Bishopston in February 1987 which resulted in a serious injury to a Bishopston player, and Old Colstonians created a Courage League precedent in September 1988 by refusing to play Dings in a Gloucestershire League Division I match later that season, their protest followed a troubled fixture between the sides the previous season. The club, of course, condoned the ill-discipline with secretary Graham Troote commenting, 'The Dings committee are right behind the clean-up campaign', but added that, 'League rugby, like cup football, is harder and more robust.'

Dings Crusaders and St Mary's Old Boys contest a line-out during the 1989 Combination Cup final, won by the emerald green and blacks 18–12.

Another Combination Cup final on 27 April 1989, this time against St Mary's Old Boys, ended in defeat as the green and blacks chalked up an 18 points to 12 win. Leading up to the game Dings had been unbeaten by a Combination side all season, but despite a near-monopoly of line-out possession and pushing their opponents back yards in the scrum, St Mary's tackling was superb. Kevin Spencer scored all of the Crusaders points; 1 try, 2 penalties and 1 conversion.

Steve Lloyd, who was captain of Dings when he was sentenced to eighteen months' imprisonment for assaulting a Bishopston player during a match in 1987, had completed his sentence and played in the final. Yatton, Oldfield Old Boys and Keynsham were beaten on the route to the final before an epic 9–9 encounter with Old Redcliffians in the semi-final, won by Dings by virtue of the only try scored. Despite their 18–12 defeat to St Mary's in the Combination Cup final, Dings deservedly retained the Merit Table title, the loss at the Memorial Ground being their solitary reverse in the competition. Significantly, Dings inflicted the only defeats on Oldfield Old Boys, who finished second

Scrum-half Kevin Spencer receives protection from number eight Sammy Stride as he collects the ball from the scrum during the 13–6 victory over St Mary's Old Boys, October 1986.

in the table. Now playing in the same Gloucestershire I league as St Mary's, Dings drew 10–10 with their longstanding rivals as Crusaders finished as runners-up to Drybrook, and a place above the Old Boys on points difference. Ten games had produced 7 wins, 1 draw and 2 defeats.

The disappointment of losing to Avonmouth 6–9 after extra time in the 1990 Combination Cup final – a second final defeat in two years – and a third place finish (Oldfield, St Mary's and Avonmouth inflicting the only defeats) in the Merit Table was tempered by a wholly successful league campaign, when following two successive seasons as runners-up promotion was finally attained. The only defeat in the ten-match 1989/90 season came in March, when Gloucester Old Boys won by 20 points to 6 at Lockleaze. Dings finished as champions in Gloucestershire I scoring 190 points with 103 conceded, as the final league game of the season, a resounding 24 points to 3 victory over St Mary's Old Boys at Landseer Avenue, clinched the title.

Dings third and final season in Gloucestershire League Division I saw, for the first time, the production of a matchday programme for the home game against Widden Old Boys on 23 September 1989. The editor, Bob Beynon, gave a brief history of the club and its origins and devoted a page to Dings' junior teams. In October, all those associated with Dings, and indeed the local rugby world, were saddened to learn of the untimely death of one of the club's legendary characters, Steve Dudley Butcher. 'Butch' joined Dings in 1972 and played 456 games for the club, 326 at First XV level. Club captain from 1983 to 1985, he was awarded his cap in 1983 and finished his playing career at Vikings level. Three matches played on Sunday, 25 February 1990 at Lockleaze in memory of Steve featured past and present members of Dings Crusaders and the Bristol Combination.

A creditable third place finish behind Spartans and Whitehall in Dings first season (1990/91) in the Gloucestershire/Somerset league resulted in 6 wins, 1 draw and 3 defeats against the two clubs that finished above them and Oldfield. In the Merit Table it was another third place finish behind Avonmouth and Whitehall, and as in the league, just three games were lost.

In March 1991, for the third year in succession Dings reached the Bristol Combination Cup final. Beaten finalists on their previous two visits to the Memorial Ground, this time the Crusaders overcame Clifton Wanderers by 21 points to 11 to lift the cup for the first time in five years. Charlie Cone, a late replacement for injured captain Gary Peters, scored two tries in the match.

Dings Crusaders Third XV, September 1990. From left to right, back row: Dave Britton, Steve Fionda, Nigel Weston, Aaron Waltho, -?-, Brian Winter, John Wilde, Dave Lyons. Front row: -?-, Mark Escott, Pete Boyes, Gerald Williams, Alan Mills, Nick Sheppard, Dave Norman.

Dings Crusaders Under-15s lost 9–10 to Clifton in the 1991 Gloucestershire Cup final. From left to right, back row: Jake Lloyd, Jamie Blyth, Mike Jefferies, Tony Jefferies, Daniel Austin, Matt Howlett, Phil Goodridge, Ross Henderson, Kevin Shipway, Scott McArthy, Adrian Jackson, Jeremy Clark, Bob Beynon, Dave Lucas. Front row: James Howarth, Simon Bishop, Tim Sperring, Jamie Britt, James Thompson, Mark Lucas, Matthew Lloyd, Barry Chester, Graham Flanders, Matt Palfrey.

Expectations for the forthcoming 1991/92 season were high as the Combination Cup holders triumphed in the pre-season North Bristol invitation fifteen-a-side tournament, defeating Whitehall 7–3 in the final, but it was to be a mid-table finish in both the league and the Merit Table.

For the start of the 1992/93 season the International Rugby Football Board introduced a change to the points scoring system when the value of a try changed to 5 points, whilst penalty and drop goals remained at 3 points. Dings completed the league season in third place and topped the Merit Table once more, with a number of crucial victories coming towards the end of the season. Two wins over Merit Table holders Old Redcliffians and a vital 13–9 success against Whitehall sent them clear of the chasing pack; with a 45–7 thrashing of Old Sulians in the last game of the season confirming Dings as champions. At the season-end presentation evening captain Steve Lloyd received a brand new *Evening Post* Merit Table trophy – which the winning club kept for a year – and an inscribed plaque to mark their achievement, which the champions retained. In an end-of-season competition, Dings lost to Old Bristolians in the Combination Senior Sevens final.

Dings, led by Nick Seward, secured their first Imperial Sevens title in thirty-two years by beating Bristol Harlequins 28–24 in the 1993 pre-season tournament. After knocking out holders Clevedon in the first round, Dings beat Midsomer Norton, Imperial and Old Redcliffians to reach the final. The club had last won the event in 1961 under the assumed name of The Vikings – a necessary precaution since, under the strict rules of the Shaftesbury Crusade (their governing temperance body), they were not permitted to play on Sundays.

With Rob Stevens taking over as captain of the Merit Table champions, the 1993/94 season started promisingly for Dings as they opened their league campaign with a resounding 40 points to 0 defeat of Thornbury and remained undefeated in the league during the course of the season. Throughout the season, Dings and St Mary's Old Boys had been locked together at the top of the Gloucestershire/Somerset league and it was a fitting finale that saw the two teams with 100 per cent records meet to determine which would be promoted. St Mary's occupied the top spot by virtue of their superior points

Dings Crusaders, 1992. Left to right, back row: Noel Beresford, Aaron Waltho, Clive Beake, Dave Britton, Richard Marsden, Dave Skuse, Andy Mogg, Jim Appleton, Kevin Davies, Rob Stevens. Front row: Errol McKenzie, Darren Lloyd, Bob Beynon (chairman), Steve Lloyd (captain), Greg Howell (coach), Derek Thatcher, Nick Seward, Gareth Lloyd. In front: the Oggy Man.

Dings Vikings, Bristol Combination Senior seven-a-side tournament winners, 1994. From left to right: Nick Seward (captain), Kevin Spencer, Darren Lloyd, Patrick Gopie, Kevin Davies, Simon Knight, Gary James, Derek Thatcher, Aaron Waltho, Dave Britton.

difference, and the promotion decider at Lockleaze was dominated for most of the 80 minutes by St Mary's but it was Dings' resilience and determination that won the day when winger Darren Lloyd went over for a last-minute try to secure a 22 points to 19 victory. That final try of the season ensured 12 wins from 12 games with 262 points scored and 100 against. Despite losing just one of their thirteen qualifying games to closest rival Cleve – a Combination Cup match – Dings added the *Evening Post* Merit Table in a season of remarkable achievement. At the end-of-season Bristol Combination Sevens tournament Dings carried off their fourth trophy when they beat Old Bristolians 31–5 in the final.

Despite the undoubted success of trophies won, the season ended with Dings again called before the Gloucestershire RFU disciplinary committee to explain their poor record, with six players sent off during the season. The committee took into account the disciplinary record over the past three seasons – fourteen ordered off – before banning the club for two weeks.

Dings celebrated their first home match at Western Counties level with a devastating eight-try performance against Drybrook at Landseer Avenue, winning by 48 points to 12. Only three defeats were suffered during the 1994/95 season and a third place was a creditable finish. Victories over Thornbury 28–11, Hornets 26–5, Avonmouth Old Boys 29–3 in the quarter-final and Keynsham 27–3 in the semi-final propelled Dings to another

Combination Cup final, this time against Clevedon. Dave Britton and Darren Lloyd scored tries, with left-wing Lloyd converting his own score and then added a penalty after the break to give Dings a 15 points to 3 victory at the Memorial Ground.

To round off another fine season for the club, Dings topped the *Evening Post* Merit Table for the third successive season with a 100 per cent rating. Thirteen games were played and thirteen victories achieved, with 383 points and only 67 against. The final game of the campaign to achieve the 'perfect finish', a 55 points to 5 drubbing of Bristol Harlequins, resulted in Dings becoming, at the time, only the second side in twenty-one years of the Merit Table to complete the season with a 100 per cent record. Showing remarkable consistency, Dings had failed to finish in the competition's top six on only two occasions, the last time back in 1984/85.

Dings Crusaders, Bristol Combination Cup winners, 1994/95. From left to right, back row: Floyd Waters (president), Noel Beresford (physio), Aaron Waltho, Richard Marsden, Gary Peters, Matt Norman, Mike Welling, Dave Britton, 'Sam' Thorne. Middle row: Ivor Sobey (touch judge), Bob Evans, Greg Howell (coach), Bob Beynon (chairman), Gerald Williams (secretary), Barry Grist, Colin Keynon, Ashley Williams, Martin Beake, Jason Cotton, Gary James, Derek Thatcher, Rob Stevens, John Stapleton, Ed Morrison (referee), Stan Thatcher, Chris Hearle, Patrick Gopie, Pete Huckle (touch judge). Front row: Chris Bailey (mascot), Dave Skuse, Errol McKenzie, Steve Knight, Steve Lloyd (captain), Nick Seward, Darren Lloyd, Kevin Spencer.

In 1995 Rugby Union became the last significant international sport to sanction professionalism, when the International Rugby Football Board legalised monetary payments in the game. To some, this represented an undesirable and problematic challenge to the status quo in which traditions of the game would be eroded and benefits would only accrue to a small clique of talented players. To many others the change was inevitable and overdue.

Until the beginning of February 1996 Dings had trailed leaders Keynsham by just one point as the two clubs battled for promotion from the Western Counties League. Dings had lost one game at Old Culverhasians (12–16) in October 1995, whilst Keynsham's only dropped point was in their drawn game with Devonport Services. However, by the middle of February Keynsham's title dreams were in ruins following the decision by the South West League committee to deduct the club 10 points for giving false information on a result card and fielding an ineligible player. With two matches of the season remaining Dings needed just one more point to finish clear of the chasing teams; Gloucester Spartans, Penzance and Devonport Services. Ironically, Dings next fixture, and penultimate game, was against Keynsham at Lockleaze, which, with a 15 points to 3 victory confirmed Dings as champions – all of the points coming from the boot of Dave Britton. The championship-winning campaign was completed in fine style with an emphatic win at Bideford by 24 points to 5 – with tries from Errol McKenzie, John Atkins and Dave Skuse, and three penalties and a conversion by Britton.

The 1996 Combination Cup finalists, Dings Crusaders and St Mary's Old Boys, had both won their respective leagues (Western Counties and Gloucestershire–Somerset) and in a close game watched by over 2,000 spectators Dings emerged victorious by 10 points to 8 to retain the cup thanks to a six-minute spell which produced a Dave Britton penalty and an Errol McKenzie try which Britton converted from the touchline. The route to the final saw Dings beat Bristol Saracens 43–6, Cleve 22–12, and Weston Hornets 25–5 in the semi-final. As a result of winning the Bristol Combination Cup Dings were invited to play Gloucester Spartans – who had won the Gloucestershire Combination Cup – in a play-off match to decide which club would gain entry to the following season's Pilkington Cup, as the county of Gloucestershire had been given an additional place in the competition. Dings hoped to follow Old Redcliffians as only the second Bristol Combination club to play in English rugby's premier knock-out competition, but were defeated 14–3 against play-off opponents Gloucester Spartans. In the County Cup, victories over Drybrook (57–11), Cinderford (30–10) and Bream (42–11) set up a semi-final visit to Gloucester Old Boys where the home team triumphed by 20 points to 9. It was another case of 'almost' as the Dings ended as Combination Senior Sevens runners-up to the University of Bristol.

There was a remarkable achievement in January 1996 by one of Dings' stalwarts, when during a game for Dings Vikings against Broad Plain Thirds at Lockleaze First team fly-half Nick Seward set a remarkable club record when he scored ten tries in an 86–0 victory.

For the 1996/97 season teams first played each other on a home and away basis in the league, and Dings' opening game in South West II was an encouraging 23–23 draw at Taunton, but the first league win of the new season didn't materialise until the beginning of October when Gordon League were defeated 44–17, although Old Richians had already been beaten 44–36 in the inaugural National Intermediate Cup competition. Twelve wins and eight defeats with two drawn games earned a fifth-place finish in the first season in the higher league. However, it was to be semi-final disappointment in both of the local cup competitions. Dings beat Avonmouth 37–6 in the quarter-final of the Combination Cup before succumbing to Keynsham 46 points to 20 in the semi-final of the competition, whilst in the Gloucestershire County Cup they were defeated 17–18 in a semi-final thriller at Matson.

Success in 1997/98 came courtesy of the Under 17s who won the the Bristol Junior Combination Sevens tournament.

Dings, in 1998/99, achieved their best finish, second place, since promotion three years earlier following a season-long tussle with Cinderford for the top spot of the South West II league. Indeed, Crusaders were the only side to inflict a league defeat, 12–10, on the champions who finished 6 points ahead of Dings after twenty-two matches. With wins over Cirencester (86–18), St Mary's Old Boys (29–10), Gordon League (18–5), Combe Down (26–16) and Cranbrook (23–11), Dings progressed to the last

Bob Beynon, photographed here in 1988, had a long and distinguished association with Dings Crusaders. Growing up in Lockleaze, he attended the junior and senior schools and joined Dings as a player when he was 12. He went on to become secretary, treasurer, captain of the team's selection committee, and chairman. Bob died in July 1998.

Dings Crusaders, Bristol Combination Cup runners-up, 1998/99. From left to right, back row: Craig Pocock (match official), Nick Cantle, Jamie Winter, Richard Marsden, Mike Jefferies, Mike Welling, Trevor Sealey, Mark Davies, Richard Glyn-Jones (match official), Rob Stevens. Third row: Floyd Waters, Ray Bowden, Mark Woodrow, James Luck, Matthew Lloyd, Gary James, Tim Davies, Noel Beresford, Andy Weymouth (match official). Second row: Steve Lloyd, Toby Oldham, Simon Knight, John Davies, Dave Lucas. Front row: Tony Whitmarsh (sponsor), Jerry Westlake, Mark Lucas, Jason Cotton (captain), Darren Lloyd, Karl Venn, Nick Seward. In front: Gavin Taylor, Luke Plummer, Josh Lloyd.

sixteen of the NPI Cup to be defeated by South West I leaders Barnstaple 8–11. Keynsham were beaten 36–16 in the Combination Cup semi-final, and despite a late Dings comeback in the final they were narrowly beaten 27–29 by Weston Hornets.

Now firmly established in the South West II division, a fourth-place finish in 1999/2000 set the foundation for the club's next drive forward after four seasons of consolidation. Following a number of runners-up shields obtained during the 1990s, in 2000 Dings Crusaders won the Combination Senior Sevens tournament again, defeating Aretians 42–7. An indication of the strength in depth throughout the club was evident when Dings Colts reached the semi-final of the inaugural Bristol Colts Cup, losing 16–22 to Clifton.

The 2000/01 season was another remarkable one for the club as the First team finished as champions of the South West II League, gaining promotion to South West League I, and also reached the final of the Combination Knock-Out Cup. However, it was not only the First XV who were amongst the honours as Dings Seconds finished top of the Bristol Combination Second Team Merit Table, whilst the Thirds were champions of the Third Team Merit

Table (Division 1) with a 100 per cent record: played 19, won 19; points for 979, against 134.

The season began well for the senior side as Ivybridge were beaten 44 points to 7 in the opening game, followed by an impressive home demolition of Clevedon by 73 points to 0 and a 32–7 away win at Hornets. Two defeats before the end of October (against Stroud and Cheltenham North) were the only two reversals until a January defeat at Matson. Recovering quickly, Cheltenham North were comprehensively beaten 58–10 in the next game. Dings then went on an unbeaten run until the end of the season overcoming old rivals St Mary's Old Boys 13–3, and Ivybridge 36–0 in the penultimate match of the campaign. The South West II title and promotion was confirmed with the 31–3 victory over St Austell at Landseer Avenue, with tries from Karl Venn (2), Darren Lloyd and Gary James, and Mark Woodrow kicking a conversion and 3 penalties as Dings completed their league programme.

The season's finale, the Combination Cup final, once again saw Dings Crusaders face their old rivals St Mary's Old Boys in the pursuit of a major

Dings Crusaders, Bristol Combination Senior Sevens runners-up, 1996. From left to right, back row: Noel Beresford, Chris Hearle, Nick Chinn, Dave Britton, Simon Knight, Tony Knight, James Luck, Darren Lloyd. Front row: John Stapleton, John Aitken, Nick Seward, Gary James, Karl Venn.

Dings Crusaders players celebrate promotion from South West II League after defeating St Austell 31 points to 3 in the final game of the 2000/01 season.

Jerry Westlake, Joe Fletcher and Vince Murrell leave the field to applause from the St Austell players and match referee following Dings' promotion from South West II League in 2001.

Dings Crusaders, Bristol Combination Cup runners-up, 2000/01. Match officials from left to right, back row: Mark Summerhayes, Craig Pocock, Andy Weymouth, Mark Doran. Fourth row: Chris Hearle, Bob Hesford (coach), Scott Mitchard, James Luck, Joseph Fletcher, Mike Jefferies, Vince Murrell, Charlie Farley, Gary James, Noel Beresford, James Winter. Third row: Karl Venn, Trevor Sealey, Paul Fincken, Nick Seward, Gary Leadbetter, Rob Stevens, Mark Davies. Second row: Ray Bowden, Steve Lloyd, Errol McKenzie, Steve Knight, Darren Lloyd, Mark Woodrow, John Davies. Front row: Josh Lloyd, Anton Welling, Floyd Waters (chairman), Jerry Westlake (captain), Luke Plummer.

trophy. St Mary's, the holders of the Cup, were making their eleventh final appearance, having been winners on eight of these occasions, whilst it was Dings' ninth appearance with five wins. The two clubs had met twice previously in a final, each gaining one win. Dings' path to the final was achieved with wins against Whitehall (18–0), Old Redcliffians (20–9), and a 35–7 semi-final victory over Southmead. However, it was St Mary's who took the trophy, for the ninth time, winning by 20 points to 8.

If an illustration of what it means to be a Dings Crusaders player is required, then probably no one epitomises that spirit more than Brian Winter who represented the club a record 1,121 times. Brian made his Dings debut when he was 18, having played rugby at Lockleaze School, because 'a lot of my friends on the estate were playing rugby'. Commenting in 2001 after chalking up 1,000 appearances Brian said, 'When I joined, Dings were the same as they are now – one big family. You weren't a First, Second, Third or Fourth team player, just a member of Dings.' Like many others, Brian stayed loyal to the club and never considered leaving, and once his playing days were over

Brian Winter receives applause on the occasion of his 1,000th appearance for Dings Crusaders in 2001. To mark the auspicious event a Bristol XV played a Dings Crusaders XV at their Lockleaze home. Brian began his rugby career with Dings in 1962 completing 1,121 games for the club before his retirement from the game in 2005.

he remained deeply involved with the club, regularly attending matches. Brian died unexpectedly in 2010.

A second successive promotion was almost achieved in 2001/02 as Dings more than coped with the step up to a higher league, but just missed out when beaten 13-29 by Basingstoke in the South East v. South West play-off match, having finished second in the league to Weston-super-Mare. Seven defeats from twenty-two league matches wasn't quite promotion standard. The Second and Third teams continued their domination of the local rugby Merit Tables, with both sides winning their respective divisions for the second season in succession. Second XV captain Craig Arathoon and Third's skipper Tim Hughes received the trophies at the presentation evening at Gordano RFC. However, it was felt that it would be beneficial to try and bridge the gap in the standard of play between the First team and the Seconds, and the decision was made that the following season the Second XV would compete in the West of England Merit Table (Northern Section), playing against Second teams from the likes of Clifton, Keynsham and Weston-super-Mare. The

Dings Crusaders players in jubilant mood following their 18–15 victory over Berry Hill, which clinched promotion to National League 3 (South) in 2003.

Thirds would move up to the Second Team Merit Table III with the Fourths/ Veterans joining the Thirds Merit Table.

The 2002/03 league season, probably the most momentous in Dings Crusaders history, began with an 8–14 reversal at Truro, but a series of wins from September to December, including a 44–21 victory over Reading, and just one further defeat, 17–25 versus Keynsham, resulted in Dings heading the South West I table as 2003 began. With another crucial victory over nearest rivals Reading in January, Dings lost only one more game, against Cheltenham in February, for the remainder of the season. Victories included a 30–17 defeat of Truro and a 27–20 away win at Clifton in March. With Berry Hill beaten 18–15 on the final Saturday of the season Dings secured the vital points to maintain that 1-point lead over Reading, who had also won their last match. Dings' playing record as Champions was: played 22, won 19, drawn 0, lost 3; points for 463, against 291. For the first time in its 106-year-history Dings Crusaders would be competing in the fourth tier of English Rugby. Further success was achieved with the lifting of the Combination Senior Sevens trophy, beating Clifton 22–21 in the final, but there was disappointment in the Gloucestershire Cup final when Dings lost 42–11 against Lydney at Kingsholm.

8

FOURTH TIER
OF ENGLISH RUGBY

Since the league structure was introduced in 1987, Dings Crusaders gained five promotions between 1990 and 2003 to enter the National leagues for the first time, when they were promoted to National Division Three South for the 2003/04 season. The early part of the season witnessed a promising Powergen Cup run with victories over Westcombe Park 21–8 and Sutton 38–25, before losing narrowly at home in the third round to Otley 3–10, who were then beaten 27–10 by visitors Bristol. What a home tie that would have been for the Dings if they could have overcome Otley.

However, in the League Dings finished in the relegation places, with 8 wins, a draw and seventeen defeats from 26 games, but were spared demotion by the demise of Wakefield, who had initially been relegated from National Division 2. Despite the difficulties of adjusting to National League rugby, Dings finished the season on a high note – avoiding relegation, however it was achieved, was deemed to be a success – by defeating Coney Hill 31–26 at Kingsholm in the final to win the Gloucestershire Cup, for the first time, and winning the Bristol Combination Senior Sevens for a second successive year, beating Clevedon 35–26 in the final.

An inprovement in the final league position saw Dings complete their second National League season with a mid-table finish in 2004/05 with 13 wins from 26 games played. At the end of the campaign Bob Hesford, head coach for five seasons, stood down after masterminding Dings rise from South West Division 2 (West) to National League 3 (South). Awarded the 'Freedom of the Dings', the honour didn't apparently entitle him to free drinks at the bar! Front-row forward Paul Johnstone, who became the new head coach, was joined by Darren Lloyd in the management set-up. Looking to win the Bristol & District Senior Sevens trophy for a third successive year, Dings were thwarted in their attempt as Clifton beat them in the final.

Dings Crusaders Fourth XV (Vikings), Bristol Combination Third XV Merit Table 1 Champions, 2005/06. From left to right, back row: Errol McKenzie, Dan Perry, Terry Webb, Jake Whiteside, Chris Lane, Mark Walsh, Nick Chinn, Pete Boyes, Dave Carradine, Tim Davies, Julian Henson, David Rees, Dave Tomlin, Steve Hawkesby, Derek Thatcher (manager). Front row: Mike Moran, Lee Beesmore, Gavin Taylor, Alan Phillips (captain), Adam Chaplin, Dave Wheeler.

With the First XV consolidating their National League status in 2005/06 with a second successive eighth-place finish, Dings Knights won the 2nd XV South West Merit Table, Dings Vikings topped their Merit Table, suffering just one defeat, whilst Dings Warriors ended the season as runners-up in the Third XV Table 1.

During the summer of 2006 a new coaching structure was put in place with an empahsis not only on the First XV but also on the emerging players who were playing for the Knights, Thirds and Fourths. With a summer of recruitment of some very promising youngsters Dings started the season, the fourth in the National League, optismtic that a top-five placing was possible, so it was with some disappointment that another mid-table finish resulted. An extended run in the EDF Cup saw Dings beat Richmond 24–6, Macclesfield 19–10, before losing in the fourth round to London Welsh 5–32. A more successful cup campaign came at the end of the season when Cinderford were defeated 9–8 in a closely contested Gloucestershire Cup final, courtesy of two Dan Quartley penalties and a Waylon Gasson drop goal.

A sixth place in 2007/08 was Dings Crusaders highest finish to date and a club record number of points, 67, in the National leagues. It was a fairly typical season for Dings with home form comparable to any side in the league, but away from Lockleaze the record was once again poor. Mark

UNDER 17'S 2007/08

Dings Crusaders Under-17s, 2007/08. From left to right, back row: Martin Beake (coach), Callum Peters, Lewis Blackwell, Scott Weston, Ricky Thomson, Ben Oaten, Tyler James, Dan Cole, Mike Norman, Shaun Newport, Alan Phillips (coach). Front row: Mark Boyes, Troy Roseway, Simon Francombe, Dean Hunt, George Sparrow, Liam Ford, Callum Bartlett, Luke Rundle.

Jefferies celebrated his last game before retiring when he led Dings to their third Gloucestershire Cup triumph in five years at The Hayfield, Cleve. Dings dominated the game against longstanding rivals St Mary's Old Boys with eight tries from Bufton, Dempsey, Jones, Murrell, Panaho, Read, Wheeler and Wright-Hider, and three conversions and a dropped-goal by Read giving a resounding 49 points to 17 victory.

Dings Crusaders Knights took on probably their strongest fixture list ever but managed to win the West of England Merit Table in 2007/08 for the second time, whilst the Third team continued to compete in the local Second team Merit Table, coming a very close second to Thornbury. With the Colts and Junior section also going well, the whole club continued to flourish.

The 2008/09 season was Dings Crusaders sixth consecutive in National Division Three South, making them the longest-serving club in that division. It began in unusual fashion with a first round Gloucestershire County Cup match at home against South West II West side Cheltenham at the end of August, who were thrashed 62–6. Remarkably, the first league match of the season at home to Canterbury was then postponed due to a waterlogged pitch! After the false start, the league campaign finally got underway a week later against Barking at Lockleaze, which saw a comfortable 30–13 victory for the Dings.

Cover of the programme for the 2008 Gloucestershire County Cup final between Dings Crusaders and St Mary's Old Boys, played at The Hayfield, Cleve's ground.

Dings Crusaders players celebrate victory over St Mary's Old Boys by 49 points to 17. It was the club's third Gloucestershire Cup triumph in five years. Vince Murrell, right, holds the Man of the Match trophy.

The scoreboard and video suite, with Lockleaze School in the distance, were familiar sights at Landseer Avenue, Dings Crusaders' home for nearly seventy years.

Dings Crusaders Colts, 2009/10. From left to right, back row: Alex Guest, James Raymond, Josh Robbins, Asa Williams, Dan Morris, Joe Hawkesby, James Oakley, Ricky ?, Kai Berg, Dan Cole, Ceri Fearnley, Nathan Moore, -?-, Adam Belsten, Marc Fitzgerald, Josh Lloyd. Front row: -?-, George Sparrow, Dean Hunt, Callum Peters, Mitch Smith, Troy Roseway, Scott Weston (captain), Lewis Blackwell, Santino Monsostori, Liam Ford, Bradley Roseway, -?-.

The EDF Energy National Trophy was a cup competition which ran from 2006 to 2009 for the 118 clubs of the RFU from National Division One and below, and in its final season (2008/09) Dings embarked on an amazing cup run which began in October when Taunton Titans were beaten 61–18. This was followed by a 24–17 victory over Ealing Trailfinders, before Westcombe Park were beaten 40–3 in the third round. The fourth-round draw provided National Three South side Dings with a home tie against the National One leaders Leeds Carnegie, favourites to win the trophy, who boasted a 100 per cent record from nineteen games.

Dings had previously entertained Leeds' fellow first division sides Otley (in 2003) and London Welsh (in 2007) in the same competition, but many at Lockleaze considered this game to be the biggest in their club's history. In preparation for the larger than normal crowd, temporary stands were erected, the gymnasium converted into a temporary bar, and additional toilets installed in order to accommodate a crowd of way above the average gate of 200 to 300. However, a cup giant-killing didn't materilise, as the full-time professionals from Yorkshire scored an avalanche of tries against their totally amateur hosts, scoring nine tries in a 59–0 victory. Leeds went on to reach the final of the competition, where they were defeated 23–18 by Birmingham Moseley.

Having disposed of Cleve by 32 points to 11 in the Gloucestershire Cup semi-final, Dings met Cinderford in the final on 7 April 2010 at the Prince of Wales Stadium in Cheltenham. Outplayed on the night, Cinderford, the reigning cup holders, were comprehensively defeated 32–10.

The 2010 Combination Cup semi-finals saw holders Clifton defeated 25–17 at home by Dings with Avonmouth Old Boys overcoming Cleve 14–10 to set up another encounter between the long-established rivals. However, the underdogs caused an upset on the night as Avonmouth defeated Dings Crusaders Knights 14–0 in the final, the match refereed by Natalie Amor, the first woman to officiate in a Combination Cup final.

The Bristol Combination Merit Table competition signed off in style at the end of the 2009/10 season with a final presentation evening at Dings Crusaders' clubhouse. Introduced ten years previously to provide a structured and competitive environment for Second, Third and Fourth XVs, these leagues had become an unexpected victim of their own success. The Gloucestershire RFU had taken note of the competition's popularity and introduced for the 2010/11 season a county-wide Reserves League, which swallowed up the Bristol Merit Tables. Dings Crusaders Vikings (Fourths) finished top of Merit Table Three as the competition bowed out.

Dings Crusaders lifted the Combination Cup for the first time since 1996 with a 36–18 victory over Weston at the Memorial Stadium in 2011, but had to come from behind twice before securing their sixth cup final success.

Dings Crusaders won their fourth Gloucestershire County Cup in 2010 when they defeated Cinderford 32–10 in the final at Cheltenham.

Having beaten Clifton 20–13 in the semi-final Crusaders' head coach Dave Hilton, the former Bristol and Scotland prop, had prepared his side to go the distance and always believed that his team would come good in the later stages of the contest because of the overall strength of his squad. Tries from Sheldon Stevens, Gavin Curry, Adam Bellamy, Neil Dipple and Sam Caven, with three penalties and a conversion from Steve Plummer provided the winning scores. This was Dings fourth final appearance since lifting the trophy in 1996 – all three previous attempts had ended in defeat. So it was fitting that former club captain James Luck, who suffered heartache in 1999, 2001 and 2010, came off the bench for Dings to make it fourth time lucky this time around.

Bristol Combination's Veterans tournament for players over the age of forty was won by Dings Crusaders in three successive seasons: 2009/10, 2010/11 and 2011/12. In fact, these were the only years that the competition was held and Dings are the proud permanent owners of the trophy.

The in-depth playing strength at Dings Crusaders was once again demonstrated in 2011/12, when Dings Knights won the Gloucestershire Reserve League (Premier Division) with 13 wins and 2 defeats in a fifteen-game campaign, the Thirds (Warriors) finishing top of their league (Reserve League South 1) winning fourteen of their seventeen games, and the Fourths (Vikings) achieving fourth place in Reserve League South 2.

In a tremendous 2013 Charles Saunders Combination Cup final, Old Redcliffians battled back to defeat Dings by 35 points to 28 at the Memorial Ground. Dings Knights also just missed out on the honours finishing a credible second to Clifton II in the Gloucestershire Reserve League (Premier Division).

It is not easy to ascertain the exact number of matches that have taken place between Dings Crusaders and Clifton XVs over the years, but early records show that Dings played Clifton Seconds in February 1902 at Westbury Road, and Clifton Thirds on The Downs in 1909. The late 1990s saw a decline in the fortunes of Clifton, their low point being relegation to South West I in 2002, and the following season they could only manage sixth place as Dings Crusaders gained promotion. However, when Clifton did return to the National League in 2006 following Dings' elevation three years earlier, the stage was set for some epic encounters to establish rugby supremacy in the Bristol area. To add a little more interest to the encounters with Dings' nearest and dearest rivals, Darren Lloyd, the former Dings winger, joined Clifton's coaching team in 2007, rising eventually to become Director of Rugby.

James Luck, captain of Dings Crusaders, and Grant Britton, Avonmouth Old Boys' captain, prepare for the 2010 Bristol Combination Cup final, with the Oggy Man also at stake. (John White Media)

Dings Crusaders, Bristol Combination Cup winners, 2010/11. From left to right, back row: Darren Yapp (coach), Josh Lloyd, Chalky Charles (manager), Luke Plummer, Gavin Curry, Gareth Lloyd, Sheldon Stevens. Third row: Millie Allen (physio), Dave Hilton (head coach), Elliot Goodman, James Oakley, Tim Brockett, Adam Bellamy, Tchad-Francois Collins, Kevin Spencer (manager). Second row: Kelly Clements (physio), Louis Osborne, Jerry Quick, Tom Knight, Matt Hudd, Darren Jefferies, James Luck. Front row: Steve Plummer, Neil Dipple, Dave Wheeler (captain), Sam Caven, James Adams, Josh Venner.

The 'Small Club from Henbury', as they are affectionately referred to at Lockleaze, were now competing in the same league, although perhaps not quite on the same level playing field as Dings, still an amateur side, competed with semi-professional Clifton – never a conscience decision to remain amateur but more borne out of necessity as Dings never had sufficient money to maintain the type of environment that has existed since professionalism was introduced to rugby in 1995. However, one thing is clear, simply throwing money and contracts at players does not guarantee promotion or even stave off relegation.

The 2013/14 season was a battle throughout to avoid relegation as the season started with three defeats in Dings' first four games. However, despite a late recovery of form which produced wins against Clifton (43–10) in March, and Launceston (36–24) on 12 April, Dings travelled to Southend on the last Saturday of the season still requiring a win to avoid the drop. A 31–12 victory against the Saxons provided the necessary points to keep the Crusaders above Launceston, Chinnor and London Irish Wild Geese to finish in eleventh position in the league.

Despite a tense end to the season Dings nevertheless went into the 2014 Combination Cup final against Clifton feeling confident, given their

Dings Crusaders played in National Leagues 2 and 3 (South) for twelve seasons between 2003 and 2015 – level four of the English Rugby Union system. National League Division 2 South was known before September 2009 as National Division Three South.

Dings Crusaders, 2011/12. From left to right, back row: Jake Lewis, Dean Brooker, Juan Enrique DaSilva-Iglesias, Joe Hawkesby, Mike Uren, Ollie Hodge, Buster Lawrence, Gareth Lloyd, Ali Crombie, James Oakley, Charlie Taylor. Third row: Darren Yapp (coach), Matt Hudd, Neil Dipple, Scott Weston, George Hooper, Callum Peters, Sheldon Stevens, Waylon Gasson, James Redmond, Alex Guest (coach). Second row: Kelly Clements (physio), Kevin Hopkins (coach), Adam Chaplin, Taylor Stevens, Dean Leadbeater, James Luck, Steve Plummer, Chris Wright-Hider, George Sparrow, Luke Small, Dan Cole, Pierre Tucker, Kevin Spencer (first team manager). Front row: Matt Wright, Harvey Skelton, Sam Cox, James Cooke, Ed Hack, Stean Williams (captain), Sam Caven, Tom Knight, Josh Lloyd, Elliott Goodman, Lewis Blackwell.

Rob Dempsey forges towards the Clifton try line, supported by James Oakley, Waylon Gasson and Joe Joyce. The expectant crowd in the 'Bear Pit' await the try. Dings won the game on 8 September 2012 by 24 points to 14. (John White Media)

Clifton entertain Dings Crusaders at Cribbs Causeway on 21 December 2012 for the first ever Friday night encounter between the two clubs. Dings Crusaders won 21–15. (John White Media)

Callum Sheedy, Jake Holcombe, Tim Turner, Ed Hack, Gareth Lloyd, Dave Wheeler, Matt Hudd, Stean Williams, Josh Lloyd and Jake Polledri reflect on why they took up rugby during a lull in play against Cambridge in January 2015. (John White Media)

Joe Joyce catches the ball cleanly at a line-out during Dings Crusaders' home fixture with Clifton on 29 March 2014, which Dings won by 43 points to 10. From left to right, on the ground: Mike Uren, Ed Hack, Sam Street (9), Josh Lloyd, James Cooke. (John White Media)

Dings Crusaders *v.* Clifton in the 2014 Combination Cup final, won by the lavender and blacks 21–16.

result against them just a few weeks previously (a 43–10 win). The league battle between the clubs that season was a draw, but the points aggregate certainly wasn't, being 60–34 in Dings' favour. Clifton had never played Dings Crusaders before in a Combination Cup final despite it being the forty-third time the competition had been held. Dings took an early lead through a well worked James Oakley try but Clifton edged back in front with two penalty goals. However, Dings turned around 8–6 at half-time thanks to a Mark Woodrow penalty. A large crowd then saw the lavender and blacks score two tries, one converted, early in the second half to take their lead to 18–8. The two sides then traded penalties before Rhys Luckwell went over for a Dings try, but Clifton held their nerve and discipline to eventually win 21–16.

It was, however, a successful season for Dings Knights as they pipped Cinderford Thirds on points difference to win the Gloucestershire Premier Reserve League, winning fourteen of their sixteen matches.

Another season-long battle in 2014/15 against relegation ended in disappointment as Dings finished well adrift of Lydney and Shelford in the other relegation places and dropped down from National Two South after winning only three of their thirty league games. The penultimate game of the season saw a humiliating reversal 62–19 at Dorking and whilst they could do nothing about where they finished, the attempt to curtail seventh-placed Chinnor to under 28 points so that Dings didn't ship over 1,000 points against them in the season failed as the visitors won by 38 points to 21 in the season's final game.

Dings went into the 2015 Combination Cup final having lost in both the 2013 and 2014 finals, but surged into a 26-point lead by the 50th minute and although Cleve fought back strongly in the final quarter, it was too late to change the destination of the silverware. Tries from Simon Hunt (two), Harry Nowell and Jake Polledri, and three Mark Woodrow conversions saw Dings' home 26–12 to end a deeply disappointing season on a relatively high note. The two finalists would find themselves together in National Three South West the following season, following Dings' relegation and Cleve's promotion.

After twelve consecutive seasons competing in National League 2 (South) it is worth recording Dings Crusaders' full playing record between 2003 and 2015: played 332, won 126, drawn 12, lost 194, points for 6,567, points against 8,150, 4 tries bonus points 69, losing bonus points 61, points 635.

Captain Ollie Reyland leads the celebrations following Dings Crusaders' victory over Cleve in the 2015 Bristol Combination Cup final. Ben Bolster, Michele Canulli, Vince Murrell, Mike Uren, Simon Hunt and Jake Holcombe prepare to join in.

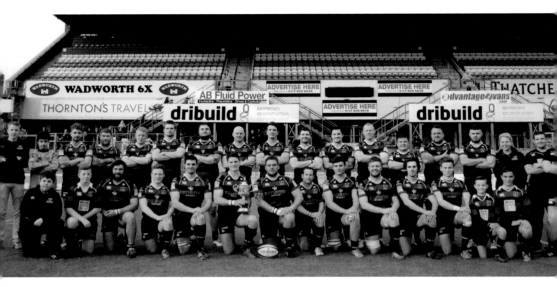

Dings Crusaders, Bristol Combination Cup winners 2014/15. From left to right, back row: Martin Wheeler, Kai Walsh, Ben Bolster, Matt Hudd, Charles Taylor, Elliot Cheesewright, Gareth Lloyd, Ed Hack, Mike Uren, Simon Hunt (coach), Sheldon Stevens, Vince Murrell (coach), Dave Wheeler, Tony Harvey, Joe Hawkesby, Laura Swarbrick (physio), Stean Williams, Andy Lyle. Front row: Ball boys: Rob Baxter, Jake Baker. Michele Canulli, Marcus Adams, Tom Knight, Olly Reyland (captain), Josh Lloyd, Mark Woodrow (coach), Jake Polledri, Jake Holcombe, Harry Nowell, Harry Tovey. Ball boys: Archie Stapleton, Mike Thatcher.

With a new squad of players Dings found it difficult adjusting to their first season outside of National League II and early season defeats set the tone for the campaign. Winning only eleven games throughout 2015/16 resulted in a nerve-wracking April with Dings beaten by Old Redcliffians, Bournemouth and Ivybridge as the season drew to its close. A second successive relegation and disastrous drop out of the National leagues was averted when the 26 points to 20 home defeat of Lydney helped the cause enormously, as Dings eventually finished in tenth position, with 53 points, the same as Newton Abbot one place below them, and 1 point better off than Old Centralians, who occupied the third relegation spot.

However, there was a notable achievement for the Under-14s side who reached the Bristol Junior Combination Cup final, being narrowly defeated by Winscombe Under-14s 0–5 in January 2016.

The 2016/17 season saw a rejuvenated Dings lose only twice, to Camborne and Old Redcliffians, in fifteen matches from September to January, and the 12–6 victory at Camborne in the final game of 2016 put Dings in pole position in the league. However, five consecutive defeats in January and February, including the crucial 15–23 home reversal against Old Redcliffians, put the

Dings Crusaders' Under-8s, 2014/15. From left to right, back row: Oliver Dell, George Towle, John King, Louis Peters-Webb, Nathan Hughes. Front row: Corey Brown, Lewis Farrant, Isaac Mahoney, George Forest. Coach: Kevin Farrant.

Dings Crusaders' Under-15s, 2016/17. From left to right, back row: -?-, Steen Maxwell, Matt Billing, Frank Godfrey, Dexter Dawes, Lewis Chant, Lewis Mills, Jake Baker, Reece Oliver, Charlie Reed, George Quartley, Max Grant, Derek Thatcher, Dan Quartley. Middle row: Shramake Waberi, Alfie Davie, Lewis Baker. Front row: John Seymour, Liam Gardiner, Thierry King, Deago Bailey, Michael Thatcher, Archie Stapleton, Anthony Smith, Lewis Bullock, Cam Brown, Kieran Billing, John Stapleton.

Dings Crusaders' Under-14s, 2015/16, photographed in Dings Crusaders clubhouse. From left to right, back row: Matt Billing, Dan Quartley, Lewis Baker, George Quartley, Dexter Dawes, Lewis Mills, Derek Thatcher, Michael Thatcher, Alfie Davies, Lewis Chant, Frank Godfrey, Jake Baker, Anthony Smith, Shramake Waberi. Front row: John Stapleton, Cam Brown, Thierry King, John Seymour, Kieran Billing, Lewis Bullock, Archie Stapleton, Max Mills, Reece Oliver, Steen Maxwell, Max Grant.

brakes on Dings automatic promotion ambition. March, however, saw a return to winning ways as the Crusaders went through the month undefeated and on 1 April Dings took a giant step towards claiming second place and a spot in the play-offs as they beat Hornets 44–22 and rivals Camborne and Ivybridge both lost. Needing only a single win from the final two games, Dings clinched a play-off place with fine victories at Ivybridge (23–17) and a 76–10 thumping of Launceston at Lockleaze in the final league game of the season.

With the team with the best playing record, hosting the match, Dings Crusaders travelled to Wimbledon, runners-up in the National League Three (London and South East), to contest the end-of-season play-off for promotion to National League II South. However, the first season at the club's new home at Shaftesbury Park would see Dings still competing in National League III (re-named South West Premier league for 2017/18) as Wimbledon triumphed by 50 points to 5, Dings' solitary score coming from replacement prop Josh Lloyd.

Ben Bolster, Sylvan Edwards, Tom Knight, Matt Smith, Connor Phillips and Chris Wright-Hider emerge from the dressing rooms for one of the last matches played at Landseer Avenue, the National 3 (South West) game against Salisbury on 25 March 2017, won by Dings 54–21.

Dings Crusaders line-up for the final home game of the 2016/17 season, which resulted in a resounding 76 points to 10 victory over Launceston. From left to right, back row: Jason Forster (head coach), Charlie Taylor, Harry Tovey, Martin Wheeler, Ben Bolster, Matt Smith, Gavin Curry, Ray Chase, Tom Knight, Matt Wright, George Nowell, Luke Arscott (backs coach). Front row: George Hooper, Jake Holcombe, Sylvan Edwards, Marlon Dorsett, Ricky Jones, Stean Williams (captain), Paul Fincken, Connor Phillips, Ashely Challenger, Steve Plummer.

9

SHAFTESBURY PARK

Dings Crusaders RFC moved to their new Lockleaze home for the commencement of the 1948/49 season and over the years the Landseer Avenue ground became part of local, and latterly national, rugby folklore. There cannot be many, if any, opposition teams who relished the thought of an away trip to Dings and the 'friendly' welcome awaiting them from the occupants in the 'Bear Pit', the covered area outside the clubhouse on the bottom touch. At times it really did feel like Fortress Dings.

However, the facilities at Landseer Avenue did not reflect the level at which the club were playing and, despite a preferred wish to remain at Lockleaze, in 2001 Dings began their search for an alternative site to call home as they looked to flourish both on and off the field, requiring a new ground and facilities to reflect their playing status. In 2011 the Trustees and Executive Committee of the Lockleaze Recreation Ground considered a proposal for the club to move to Almondsbury but it was left to club members to make the decision to leave Lockleaze or not, which resulted in a very close vote rejecting the move.

In 2014 it was announced that the club would be moving from their Lockleaze home to Frenchay Park Road, where a new ground would be built, as planning permission had been granted by South Gloucestershire Council to build houses on their base at Landseer Avenue. The decision meant that Dings, working in partnership with Redrow Homes, could now afford to fund a new £8 million ground on 26 acres of land opposite the former Frenchay Hospital.

The new home of Dings Crusaders RFC, Shaftesbury Park – the name pays homage to the Shaftesbury Crusade – provides a new community sports facility comprising three full-size rugby pitches – one of which will be an

Dings Crusaders' ground, Landseer Avenue, in the late 1970s. The original white roofed huts are clearly visible, with the Shaftesbury Crusade building to the right.

Shaftesbury Park, Dings Crusaders new home from October 2017. (John White Media)

artificial surface – four grass junior rugby pitches (including floodlighting to two pitches), a clubhouse building with community sports hall, eight changing rooms, weight training room and gymnasium, spectator seating and viewing area, function/meeting rooms and a club shop.

New homes will have to be found for the memorabilia and trophies that have adorned the Landseer Avenue clubhouse for many years, as well as the 'Clifton Trophy Cabinet' containing souvenirs and mementos brought back to Lockleaze following away games against the lavender and blacks. 'Props Corner', that almost holy place to the right of the clubhouse bar will also re-locate to Shaftesbury Park, and The Oggy Man will require a new 'permanent' seat.

As Dings Crusaders prepare for a bright new future at Shaftesbury Park it is important, however, to remember the history and heritage of the club and the wonderful years spent at Lockleaze. There probably never was a better place for a Dings player to score a try than in 'Dog shit corner', and with no stinging nettles at the new ground, rampaging Dings' forwards will no longer be able to 'Push 'em in the stingers', but in the words of chairman Steve Lloyd:

> We must build on the legacy that has been left us. All club members, young and old, must ensure that the Dings' spirit that has served us so well over the last 120 years is fully recognised and respected, with everyone fully aware of the pride in representing this truly unique rugby club at all levels.

10

CLUB HONOURS AND AWARDS

HONOURS

1900/01	Bristol Junior Cup	Winners
1901/02	Bristol Combination Division II Cup	Winners
	Bristol Combination Division III Cup	Winners
1902/03	Bristol Combination Division III Cup	Winners
1909/10	Bristol Combination Division II Cup	Winners
1919/20	Bristol Combination Senior Cup	Winners
1936/37	Senior Combination Seven-a-Side	Winners
1946/47	Senior Combination Seven-a-Side	Winners
1960/61	Senior Combination Seven-a-Side	Winners
1962/63	Senior Combination Seven-a-Side	Runners-up
1972/73	Gloucestershire Cup	Runners-up
1973/74	Bristol & District Knock-Out Cup	Winners
1979/80	Bristol Evening Post Merit Table	Champions
1983/84	Bristol & District Senior Sevens	Runners-up
1985/86	Bristol & District Knock-Out Cup	Winners
1987/88	Bristol Evening Post Merit Table	Champions
	Gloucestershire League I	Runners-up
1988/89	Bristol & District Knock-Out Cup	Runners-up
	Bristol Evening Post Merit Table	Champions
	Gloucestershire League I	Runners-up
1989/90	Gloucestershire League Division I	Champions
	Bristol & District Knock-Out Cup	Runners-up
1990/91	Bristol & District Knock-Out Cup	Winners
1992/93	Bristol & District Senior Sevens	Runners-up
	Bristol Evening Post Merit Table	Champions

1993/94	Gloucestershire/Somerset League	Champions
	Bristol & District Senior Sevens	Winners
	Bristol Evening Post Merit Table	Champions
1994/95	Bristol & District Knock-Out Cup	Winners
	Bristol Evening Post Merit Table	Champions
1995/96	Western Counties League	Champions
	Bristol & District Knock-Out Cup	Winners
	Bristol & District Senior Sevens	Runners-up
1997/98	Bristol & District Senior Sevens	Runners-up
1998/99	Bristol & District Knock-Out Cup	Runners-up
	South West II – West League	Runners-up
1999/00	Bristol & District Senior Sevens	Winners
2000/01	South West II – West League	Champions
	Bristol & District Knock-Out Cup	Runners-up
	Bristol Evening Post 2nd Team Merit Table	Champions
	Bristol Evening Post 3rd Team Merit Table	Champions
2001/02	South West I – West League	Runners-up
	Bristol Evening Post 2nd Team Merit Table	Champions
	Bristol Evening Post 3rd Team Merit Table	Champions
	Bristol & District Senior Sevens	Winners
2002/03	South West I League	Champions
	Bristol & District Senior Sevens	Winners
	Gloucestershire Cup	Runners-up
2003/04	Gloucestershire Cup	Winners
	Bristol & District Senior Sevens	Winners
2004/05	Bristol & District Senior Sevens	Runners-up
2005/06	Bristol Evening Post 3rd Team Merit Table	Champions
2005/06	South West 2nd Team Merit Table	Winners
2006/07	Gloucestershire Cup	Winners
2007/08	Gloucestershire Cup	Winners
	South West 2nd Team Merit Table	Winners
2009/10	Gloucestershire Cup	Winners
	Bristol & District Knock-Out Cup	Runners-up
	Bristol Evening Post 3rd Team Merit Table	Champions
	Bristol & District Over-40s Cup	Winners
2010/11	Bristol & District Knock-Out Cup	Winners
	Bristol & District Over-40s Cup	Winners
2011/12	Gloucestershire Reserve League Premier (Dings Knights)	Champions
	Gloucestershire Reserve League South I (Dings Warriors)	Champions

	Bristol & District Over-40s Cup	Winners
2012/13	Bristol & District Knock-Out Cup	Runners-up
2013/14	Bristol & District Knock-Out Cup	Runners-up
	Gloucestershire Reserve League Premier (Dings Knights)	Champions
2014/15	Bristol & District Knock-Out Cup	Winners
2016/17	National League III (South West)	Runners-up

CLUB PRESIDENT

1897–1930	H.M. Harris
1930–1960	H.W. Rudge
1960–1982	J.B. Steadman
1982–1991	G.F.O. Backes
1991–2012	A.F. Waters
2012–	R. Bowden

CLUB CHAIRMAN

1945–1969	L.R. Fynn
1969–1980	G.F.O. Backes
1980–1991	A.F. Waters
1991–1998	R.J. Beynon
1998–	S. Lloyd

HONORARY SECRETARY

1897–1930	H.W. Rudge
1930–1961	J.B. Steadman
1961–1966	P. Masoli
1966–1969	G.F.O. Backes
1969–1979	A.F. Waters
1979–1983	T. Denley
1983–1985	R.J. Beynon
1985–1991	G. Troote
1991–1996	G. Williams
1996–2007	R. Stevens
2007–	P. Jones

HONORARY LIFE MEMBERS

Grahame Backes	1965
Les Fynn	1969
Joe Rogers	1972
Floyd Waters	1976
John White	1979
Jim Batten	1983
Richard Hook	1983
Colin Kimmins	1983
Graham Troote	1983
Bert Angell	1985
Colin Watkeys	1985
Bob Beynon	1989
Ray Bowden	1990
Gerry Williams	1994
Chris Searle	1995
John Thorne	1995
Phil Knowles	1999
Steve Lloyd	2001
Terry Webb	2001
Richard Grant	2004
Rob Stevens	2004
Pat Clark	2006
Ivor Fackrell	2008
Jim Austin	2011
John Davies	2011
Dave Lucas	2011
Colin Lewis	2012
John Watkins	2012

CLUB CAPTAIN

1897–1900	[No record]
1901–1904	Henry Hussey
1904–1905	George Hale
1905–1906	Arthur Oatley
1906–1909	[No record]
1909–1910	J. Prideaux
1910–1914	[No record]
1914–1919	First World War
1919–1922	William T. Bryant
1922–1923	E. Payne

1923–1924	T. Matthews
1924–1925	Arthur V. Sampson
1925–1926	A. Groves
1926–1927	Arthur V. Sampson
1927–1928	E. Vale
1928–1929	Arthur V. Sampson
1929–1930	Arthur H. Portch
1930–1931	Albert Duffett
1931–1932	Arthur Payne
1932–1934	Ernest Seward
1934–1935	Joe Rogers
1935–1936	Ernest Seward
1936–1938	Frederick T. Payne
1938–1939	Arthur Payne
1939–1945	Second World War
1945–1946	Leslie Seward
1946–1947	Jack Harris
1947–1950	Harry Brooks
1950–1952	Les Fynn
1952–1953	Maurice Bryant
1956–1957	Grahame Backes
1957–1958	Alan Hudson
1955–1956	Terry Paul
1956–1957	Grahame Backes
1957–1958	Alan Hudson
1958–1959	Graham Troote
1959–1960	Brian Plumley
1960–1963	Roy Phibben
1963–1966	Colin Kimmins
1966–1967	Roy Phibben
1967–1970	Colin Kimmins
1970–1971	Jim Austin
1971–1975	Richard Hook
1975–1977	Richard Grant
1977–1978	Alan Ferris
1978–1980	Philip Knowles
1980–1982	Gerry Williams
1982–1983	Alan Ferris
1983–1985	Steve Butcher
1985–1987	Rob Stevens
1987–1989	Steve Lloyd
1989–1991	Gary Peters

1991–1993	Steve Lloyd
1993–1994	Rob Stevens
1994–1996	Steve Lloyd
1996–1997	Simon Knight
1997–1998	Steve Lloyd
1998–2000	Jason Cotton
2000–2002	Jerry Westlake
2002–2003	James Luck
2003–2007	Paul Fincken
2007–2008	Mike Jeffries
2008–2009	Mike Panoho
2009–2010	Stean Williams
2010–2011	Dave Wheeler
2011–2012	Stean Williams
2012–2014	Ed Hack
2014–2015	Olly Reyland
2015–2017	Stean Williams
2017–2018	Steve Plummer

LES FYNN SHIELD

Awarded annually to the most outstanding club member for unselfish and loyal club service. It was formerly known as the 'Crusaders Shield'.

1952–1953	Graham Troote
1953–1954	Grahame Backes
1954–1955	John Waterman
1955–1956	Harry Brooks
1956–1957	Les Fynn
1957–1958	Maurice Bryant
1958–1959	Joe Rogers
1959–1960	Stan Bryant
1960–1961	Bill Pell
1961–1962	Tom White
1962–1963	Bob Campbell
1963–1964	Jack Hucker
1964–1965	Chris Allen
1965–1966	Colin Kimmins
1966–1967	Bert Angell
1967–1968	Peter Jenkins
1968–1969	Bill Brooks
1969–1970	Floyd Waters

1970–1971	Roy Phibben
1971–1972	Stan Bryant
1972–1973	Trevor Denley
1973–1974	Richard Hook
1974–1975	Bob Beynon
1975–1976	Gordon Brown
1976–1977	'Dickie' Phillips
1977–1978	Jim Austin
1978–1979	John Thorne
1979–1980	Philip Knowles
1980–1981	Brian Rees
1981–1982	Gerald Williams
1982–1983	John Knight
1983–1984	Gary Peters
1984–1985	Terry Webb
1985–1986	Bill Bransome
1986–1987	Ray Bowden
1987–1988	Dave Lucas
1988–1989	Martin Carter
1989–1990	Brian Winter
1990–1991	Greg Howell
1991–1992	Tony James
1992–1993	Steve Lloyd
1993–1994	Noel Beresford
1994–1995	Rob Stevens
1995–1996	Barry Grist
1996–1997	John Watkins
1997–1998	John Davies
1998–1999	John Searle
1999–2000	Peter Boyes
2000–2001	Richard Grant
2001–2002	Andy Plummer
2002–2003	Neil Taylor
2003–2004	Colin Lewis
2004–2005	Jim Appleton
2005–2006	John Knight
2006–2007	Derek Thatcher
2007–2008	Mark Wright
2008–2009	Chris Lloyd
2009–2010	Mark Wright
2010–2011	Kevin Spencer
2011–2012	Mez Merriman

2012–2013	Pete Jones
2013–2014	Mike Sanigar
2014–2015	John Stapleton
2015–2016	Gareth Roberts
2016–2017	Mez Merriman

THE LORRAINE CUP

Awarded annually by the First XV to their outstanding player. The Cup is named in memory of Lorraine Carter (*née* Trusler).

1975–1976	Richard Grant
1976–1977	Gerald Williams
1977–1978	John Thorne
1978–1979	Richard Hook
1979–1980	Phil Henson
1980–1981	Alan Ferris
1981–1982	Chris Allen
1982–1983	Rob Stevens
1983–1984	Chris Lloyd
1984–1985	Steve Lloyd
1985–1986	Derek Gunningham
1986–1987	John Thorne
1987–1988	Gary Peters
1988–1989	Noel Beresford
1989–1990	Ian Westaway
1990–1991	Errol McKenzie
1991–1992	Dave Skuse
1992–1993	Mike Welling
1993–1994	Nick Seward
1994–1995	Jason Cotton
1995–1996	Aaron Waltho
1996–1997	Simon Knight
1997–1998	Steve Lloyd
1998–1999	Mike Welling
1999–2000	Simon Knight
2000–2001	Mike Jeffries
2001–2002	Stean Williams
2002–2003	Mark Woodrow
2003–2004	Paul Fincken
2004–2005	Sylvan Edwards
2005–2006	Barrie Cole

2006–2007	Chas Meddick
2007–2008	Mike Panoho
2008–2009	Orlando Stott
2009–2010	Gavin Curry
2010–2011	Tim Brockett
2011–2012	Sam Cox
2012–2013	Joe Joyce
2013–2014	Jake Holcombe
2014–2015	Michele Canulli
2015–2016	Stean Williams
2016–2017	Matt Smith

THE H.W. RUDGE SPORTSMAN CUP

Awarded annually to the most outstanding senior player for sportsmanship.

1957–1958	Graham Troote
1958–1959	Terry Annette
1959–1960	Tony Church
1960–1961	Mike Nicholls
1961–1962	Brian Plumley
1962–1963	Bert Angell
1963–1964	Floyd Waters
1964–1965	George Frampton
1965–1966	Colin Kimmins
1966–1967	George Fackrell
1967–1968	Martin Williams
1968–1969	Gordon Challenger
1969–1970	Gerald Williams
1970–1971	Pat Clark
1971–1972	John Phillips
1972–1973	Pete Jones
1973–1974	Jim Challenger
1974–1975	Richard Hook
1975–1976	'Dickie' Phillips
1976–1977	Jim Austin
1977–1978	Grahame Backes
1978–1979	Gordon Brown
1979–1980	Brian Winter
1980–1981	Colin Watkeys
1981–1982	Richard Grant
1982–1983	Alan Ferris

1983–1984	Dave Appleton
1984–1985	Chris Searle
1985–1986	Dave White
1986–1987	John Searle
1987–1988	Phil Henson
1988–1989	Dave Richards
1989–1990	Terry Webb
1990–1991	Gary Peters
1991–1992	Rob Stevens
1992–1993	Peter Boyes
1993–1994	Dave Rees
1994–1995	Tony Green
1995–1996	Tim Berry
1996–1997	Colin Kenyon
1997–1998	Mike Jeffries
1998–1999	Toby Oldham
1999–2000	James Winter
2000–2001	Chris Hearle
2001–2002	Charlie Farley
2002–2003	Vincent Murrell
2003–2004	Alan Phillips
2004–2005	Dean Leadbetter
2005–2006	Mike Trench
2006–2007	Paul Fincken
2007–2008	Martin Gallagher
2008–2009	Craig Jenkins
2009–2010	Josh Sampson
2010–2011	Alex Dancer
2011–2012	Josh Lloyd
2012–2013	Ed Wander
2013–2014	Steve Plummer
2014–2015	Tom Knight
2015–2016	Anthony Harvey
2016–2017	Jake Whiteside

ARTHUR PAYNE MEMORIAL TROPHY

Awarded annually to the most outstanding Junior player for sportsmanship.

1968–1969	Michael Hodge
1969–1970	'Dickie' Phillips

1970–1971	Alan Ferris
1971–1972	Tony Palfry
1972–1973	Ian Watts
1973–1974	(No award)
1974–1974	Rob Stevens
1975–1976	Nick Marment
1976–1977	Steve Lloyd
1977–1978	Dean Williams
1978–1979	Huw Duggan
1979–1980	Steve Hawkins
1980–1981	Steve Troote
1981–1982	Brian Sims
1982–1983	Sam Thorne
1983–1984	Derek Thatcher
1984–1985	Paul Newlands
1985–1986	Dave Hilton
1986–1987	Aaron Waltho
1987–1988	Nick Seward
1988–1989	Gregg Henderson
1989–1990	Nick Sheppard
1990–1991	Cain Hawkins
1991–1992	Steven Parkes
1992–1993	Stean Williams
1993–1994	Tom Eastman
1994–1995	Simon Watkins
1995–1996	Will Horsley
1996–1997	Mark Davies
1997–1998	Mark Woodrow
1998–1999	Paul Fincken
1999–2000	Richard Skuse
2000–2001	Dean Spencer
2001–2002	(No award)
2002–2003	(No award)
2003–2004	Simon Tsangari
2004–2005	Dave Wheeler
2005–2006	Jake Whiteside
2006–2007	Adam Chaplin
2007–2008	Luke Plummer
2008–2009	Mike Norman
2009–2010	Josh Robbins
2010–2011	Charles Taylor

2011–2012	Will Tobin
2012–2013	Joe Hawkesbury
2013–2014	Joe Dancer
2014–2015	(No award)
2015–2016	(No award)
2016–2017	Martin Wheeler

THE H.M. HARRIS MEMORIAL CUP
Henry Morris Harris was Dings Crusaders' president from 1897 to 1930.

1992–1993	Mike Haskins
1993–1994	Scott McCarthy
1994–1995	James Luck
1995–1996	Tom Eastman

BRIAN WINTER SHIELD
Awarded annually to the Junior Clubman of the year for their contribution to the Junior Section.

2011–2011	Matt Wright
2011–2012	Charlie Glover
2012–2013	Sid Harrison
2013–2014	Jake Baker
2014–2015	Archie Stapleton
2015–2016	George Gallagher
2016–2017	Lewis Bullock

CLUB CAPS
Caps were originally awarded to players who had completed 300 first team games or 500 club games. This was amended to award a cap for 300 club games, and reduced further to 250 club games.

1980	Jim Austin
	Grahame Backes
	Bob Beynon
	Gordon Brown
	Stan Bryant
	Martin Carter

Jim Challenger
Trevor Denley
Richard Grant
Phil Henson
Richard Hook
Colin Kimmins
Phil Knowles
John Phillips
Jack Steadman
Graham Troote
Floyd Waters
Gerald Williams

1981   Derek Gunningham
Michael Phillips
Colin Watkeys
Dave White
Brian Winter

1982   Chris Bailey
Jim Batten
Ray Bowden
Alan Ferris
Paul Lloyd
John Searle

1983   Dave Appleton
Jim Appleton
Noel Beresford
Steve Butcher
Pat Clark
John Peach
John Thorne
Rob Williams

1984   Geoff Darby
John Knight
Chris Searle

1985   Chris Lloyd
Andy Lyle

1986   Rob Stevens

1987   Tony James
              Steve Lloyd

1988   Dave Richards

1989   Chris Butcher
              Colin Lewis
              Gary Peters
              Sam Stride
              John Whittaker

1990   Chris Allen
              Martin Beake
              Steve Fionda
              Steve Hawkesby
              Pat Hennessy
              Roger Saunders
              Kevin Spencer
              Ian Westaway
              Nigel Weston

1991   Barry Grist
              Harry Parsons

1992   Clive Beake
              Paul Green
              Stan Thatcher

1993   Tim Berry
              Kevin Davies

1994   Tim Hughes
              Errol McKenzie
              Alan Phillips
              Derek Thatcher

1995   Paul Appleton
              Tony Green
              Sam Sparrow

1996	Nick Chinn
	Dave Skuse

1997	Nick Seward
	Lee Williams

1998	Peter Boyes
	Chris Hearle
	Colin Kenyon

1999	Bert Angell
	Gary James

| 2000 | Darren Lloyd |

2002	Ian Appleton
	Mike Haskins
	Mike Welling

2003	Roy Phibben
	John Stapleton
	James Winter

2005	Mike Jefferies
	Simon Knight
	James Luck

2006	Mark Lucas
	Rich Marsden

2007	Matthew Billing
	Richard Stone

2008	Craig Arathoon
	Tim Davies

| 2010 | Steve Davies |

| 2012 | Jerry Westlake |

| 2013 | Martin Avery |

2014   Vincent Murrell
                Patrick Parsons
                Dave Wheeler

2015   Matthew Quick
                Marcus Strafford

2016   Ed Hack
                Josh Lloyd

2017   Sylvan Edwards
                Paul Fincken
                Jerry Quick
                Mark Walsh
                Stean Williams

PRESENTATION TIES

Awarded for meritorious club service.

1968–69   Roy Phibben
                Bert Nutt

1969–70   Dave Brown
                Maurice Graham
                John Sheppard

1971–72   Jack Steadman
                'Dickie' Phillips

1972–73   Jim Batten
                Alan Llewellin
                Pete Williams

1973–74   Each member of the Combination Cup Winning XV

11

PLAYING RECORDS

LEAGUE RECORD 1987–2017

SEASON	LEAGUE	POSITION	PLAYED	WON	DREW	LOST	FOR	AGAINST	POINTS
1987/88	Gloucestershire I	2nd	10	9	0	1	153	65	18
1988/89	Gloucestershire I	2nd	10	7	1	2	150	95	15
1989/90	Gloucestershire I	1st	10	9	0	1	190	103	18
1990/91	Gloucestershire/Somerset	3rd	10	6	1	3	160	87	13
1991/92	Gloucestershire/Somerset	6th	10	6	0	4	163	142	12
1992/93	Gloucestershire/Somerset	3rd	12	6	3	3	194	128	15
1993/94	Gloucestershire/Somerset	1st	12	12	0	0	262	100	24
1994/95	Western Counties	3rd	12	9	0	3	335	124	18
1995/96	Western Counties	1st	11	10	0	1	232	87	20
1996/97	South West II (West)	5th	22	12	2	8	470	415	26
1997/98	South West II (West)	7th	22	10	1	11	442	351	21
1998/99	South West II (West)	2nd	22	17	0	5	466	222	34
1999/00	South West II (West)	4th	22	14	1	7	430	281	27
2000/01	South West II (West)	1st	22	19	0	3	604	237	38
2001/02	South West I	2nd	22	15	0	7	409	315	30
2002/03	South West I	1st	22	19	0	3	463	291	38
2003/04	National III (South)	12th	26	8	1	17	386	624	17
2004/05	National III (South)	8th	26	13	0	13	516	538	62
2005/06	National III (South)	8th	26	11	1	14	551	648	59
2006/07	National III (South)	9th	26	9	3	14	445	628	51
2007/08	National III (South)	6th	26	13	1	12	492	441	67
2008/09	National III (South)	6th	26	12	2	12	514	580	61
2009/10	National II (South)	11th	28	9	2	17	549	697	53
2010/11	National II (South)	10th	30	12	1	17	718	765	62

2011/12	National II (South)	12th	30	11	0	19	552	741	55
2012/13	National II (South)	9th	28	13	0	15	635	738	58
2013/14	National II (South)	11th	30	12	0	18	679	745	68
2014/15	National II (South)	16th	30	3	1	26	526	1009	22
2015/16	National III (South West)	10th	26	11	0	15	485	568	53
2016/17	National III (South West)	2nd	26	19	0	7	676	448	87

EVENING POST MERIT TABLE 1973–1996

SEASON	POSITION	PLAYED	WON	DREW	LOST	FOR	AGAINST	POINTS	%
1973/74	4th	27	20	1	6	524	248	41	75.93
1974/75	4th	24	17	1	6	342	167	35	72.92
1975/76	2nd	28	22	2	4	555	215	46	82.14
1976/77	5th	25	18	1	6	328	154	37	74.00
1977/78	4th	25	20	1	4	438	171	41	82.00
1978/79	2nd	23	18	0	5	406	142	36	78.26
1979/80	1st	29	24	4	1	491	147	52	89.66
1980/81	2nd	25	21	1	3	423	133	43	86.00
1981/82	6th	25	17	2	6	361	166	36	72.00
1982/83	9th	23	13	2	8	376	180	28	60.87
1983/84	6th	27	20	0	7	492	228	40	74.07
1984/85	10th	25	16	1	8	390	242	33	66.00
1985/86	3rd	27	22	2	3	488	159	46	85.19
1986/87	3rd	26	23	0	3	506	177	46	88.46
1987/88	1st	21	19	1	1	385	127	39	92.86
1988/89	1st	22	19	2	1	418	158	40	90.91
1989/90	3rd	19	6	0	3	444	93	32	84.21
1990/91	3rd	14	11	0	3	318	113	22	78.57
1991/92	6th	12	8	1	3	184	96	17	70.83
1992/93	1st	18	14	2	2	427	149	30	83.33
1993/94	1st	13	12	0	1	273	101	24	92.31
1994/95	1st	13	13	0	0	383	67	26	100
1995/96	1st	7	7	0	0	205	82	14	100

BRISTOL COMBINATION MERIT TABLES 1999–2010

SEASON	TABLE	TEAM	POSITION	PLAYED	WON	DREW	LOST	FOR	AGAINST	POINTS	%
1999/00	Second XV Table 1	2nds	3rd	16	12	0	4	515	199	40	83.33
2000/01	Second XV Table 1	2rds	1st	19	17	1	1	500	179	54	94.74
2000/01	Third XV Table 1	3nds	1st	19	19	0	0	979	134	57	100
2001/02	Second XV Table 1	2nds	1st	18	17	0	1	538	179	52	96.30
2001/02	Third XV Group A	3rds	1st	14	13	0	1	480	142	40	95.24
2002/03	Second XV Table 2	3rds	6th	18	9	0	9	282	246	35	64.81
2002/03	Third XV Group A	4ths	8th	8	1	4	3	64	101	6	25.00
2003/04	Second XV Table 2	3rds	2nd	17	15	0	2	204	118	47	92.16
2003/04	Third XV Table 1	4ths	7th	11	4	0	6	211	166	18	54.55
2004/05	Second XV Table 1	3rds	3rd	16	10	0	6	315	249	38	75.00
2004/05	Third XV Table 1	4ths	6th	10	4	0	6	150	180	18	60.00
2005/06	Second XV Table 1	3rds	2nd	22	16	2	4	293	241	56	84.85
2005/06	Third XV Table 1	4ths	1st	16	15	0	1	250	121	46	95.83
2006/07	Second XV Table 1	3rds	2nd	22	17	1	4	407	197	57	86.36
2006/07	Third XV Table 1	4ths	3rd	16	9	1	5	242	213	34	70.83
2007/08	Second XV Table 1	3rds	2nd	16	13	0	3	158	123	42	87.50
2007/08	Third XV Table 1	4ths	5th	7	3	0	4	80	75	11	52.38
2008/09	Table 1	3rds	2nd	15	11	0	4	299	234	36	80.00
2008/09	Table 3	4ths	8th	10	3	0	7	153	148	13	43.30
2009/10	Table 1	3rds	10th								
2009/10	Table 3	4ths	1st								

2ND XV WEST OF ENGLAND MERIT TABLE 2002–2008

SEASON	TABLE	POSITION	PLAYED	WON	DREW	LOST	FOR	AGAINST	POINTS	%
2002-03	Northern Section	4th	13	7	1	5	233	288	15	58
2003-04	Northern Section	3rd	16	8	2	6	426	324	18	56
2004-05	Northern Section	3rd	16	12	1	3	486	166	25	78
2005-06		1st	13	13	0	0	490	95	26	100
2006-07		5th	14	7	2	5	354	216	16	57
2007-08		1st	15	12	0	3	401	167	24	80

GLOUCESTERSHIRE RFU RESERVE LEAGUES 2010–2017

SEASON	TABLE	TEAM	POSITION	PLAYED	WON	DREW	LOST	FOR	AGAINST	POINTS	%
2010/11	Premier	2nds	3rd	16	10	0	6	461	292	56	70.00
2010/11	South I	3rds	3rd	14	11	0	3	330	191	58	82.86
2010/11	South II	4ths	4th	15	11	0	4	396	217	51	68.00
2011/12	Premier	2nds	1st	15	13	0	2	513	151	67	89.33
2011/12	South I	3rds	1st	17	14	0	3	623	147	73	85.88
2011/12	South II	4ths	4th	20	15	0	5	614	283	67	67.00
2012/13	Premier	2nds	2nd	11	8	0	3	311	145	39	70.91
2012/13	South I	3rds	6th	13	9	0	4	331	244	36	55.38
2012/13	South II	4ths	10th	6	4	0	2	163	92	-6	-20.00
2013/14	Premier	2nds	1st	16	14	0	2	598	195	72	90.00
2013/14	South I	3rds	6th	11	5	0	6	269	242	31	56.36
2014/15	Premier	2nds	3rd	10	6	0	4	315	132	33	66.00
2014/15	Bristol & District II	3rds	10th	9	4	0	5	293	248	0	0.00
2015/16	Premier	2nds	7th	3	0	0	3	58	92	-11	-73.33
2015/16	Bristol & District I	3rds	12th	7	4	0	3	198	124	-4	0.00
2016/17	Bristol & District I	3rds	4th	10	5	0	5	259	243	25	50.00

GLOUCESTERSHIRE RFU SOUTH WEST PILOT LEAGUE

SEASON	LEAGUE	TEAM	POSITION	PLAYED	WON	DREW	LOST	FOR	AGAINST	POINTS
2016/17	Pilot League	2nds	6th	14	6	0	8	219	317	19

ABOUT THE AUTHOR

Ian Haddrell attended Lockleaze School in Bristol and is the author of nine books on local history and sport. He has also written *A Bristol Soldier in the Second World War*, the story of his father's experiences in Normandy in 1944. He is a committee member of the Frampton Cotterell Local History Society and has been involved in a number of research projects for them. A keen family historian, he has been researching his ancestors for over forty years, and as a member of the Guild of One Name Studies researches all those with the surname Haddrell, and its variants, worldwide and throughout history. A member of the Western Front Association and the Gallipoli Association, he has a particular interest in the First World War.

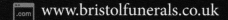